From *My* Story To *History*

LAMPS
MINISTRY
TESTIMONIES
Volume One

Contributions by LAMPS Ministry Participants

Edited and Compiled by Amber Nicole McKinzy

Published by

Our Written Lives, LLC

Cover Photography by Ann Nester and Ann's Location Photography

Edited and Compiled by Amber Nicole McKinzy
Cover and LAMPS Logo designed by Karen Reed Buller
Writing by LAMPS Ministry Participants

Dedication

For every soul wounded, broken, and on their journey to wholeness, may this book of testimonies shine light on your darkness and bring you from despair to hope!
I pray that as you read this book, you will experience personal healing and wholeness. Rise and be healed, in Jesus' Name!

Rev. Kathy McManus Corson
Founder, LAMPS Ministries

For all who need healing, and to those who view restoration as an impossibility. Don't give up on yourself. Continue to persevere! Pursue after complete healing and wholeness. You will be amazed at the supernatural work the Lord will perform in your life.

Amber Nicole McKinzy
Editor, LAMPS Ministries

Ladies **A**bused **M**entally **P**hysically **S**piritually substance sexual self

LAMPS Ministry is a traveling women's ministry based out of Summit, Mississippi, led by Rev. Kathy Corson. Conferences and services are held in various cities.

For information, email kc.lampsministry@yahoo.com or call Rev. Kathy Corson at 318.268.5442.

Contents

Acknowledgments _____ 6

Preface _____ 9

Foreword _____ 13

Introduction_____ 15

1. God's Art Piece_____ 19

2. A Covering of Grace_____ 23

3. Through the Fire _____ 35

4. A Woman After God's Heart _____ 45

5. Never Too Young _____ 67

6. From the Preacher's Home _____ 69

7. Jesus Loves Me _____ 79

8. He Made Sure I Didn't Forget _____ 87

9. I Forgave & I'm Forgiven _____ 97

10. It Saved My Life_____ 103

11. Brokenness to Wholeness _____ 105

12. Recovering Identity _____ 111

13. Scars_____ 147

Acknowledgments

First of all, thank you to Jesus Christ, the author, and finisher of my faith and story.

Betty Martin, you are an extraordinary and instrumental lady. God placed you in my life and used you to illuminate my path in a time of rejection and lack of direction, when I felt battered, bruised, and broken. I'm glad God allowed our paths to cross! Because of you, I made it through my journey from hurt to wholeness, and now to helping others heal!

Paula, my one and only daughter. You are an inspiration to me, despite being on your journey to becoming whole. You have been a blessing to my life, and a gift from God. I'm proud of you, Paula.

To everyone that contributed to this book in any capacity, Thank you! Your work will be rewarded! To the courageous women who shared your stories, you are overcomers by the blood of the Lamb and the WORD of your TESTIMONY!

Rev. Kathy McManus Corson

Founder, LAMPS Ministries

Thank you, Jesus Christ. You are the focus of my worship, the lover of my soul, and the healer and restorer of my life.

Sis. Kathy Corson. Your mentorship, friendship, and love have meant the world to me. Thank you for believing in me and seeing past my brokenness to who God has called me to be. You are a treasure.

My husband, Gene. Your faithful love and daily kindness have helped me become whole. I love you with all my heart.

My children, Amberly, Austen, & Zachery. Your lives helped to save mine. I'm forever proud of the strength and faith you exemplify.

Jessica Loftin, thank you for obeying the voice of God. You were the first person to introduce me to LAMPS.

Sis. Anna Heard and Sis. Cathy Talent. God used each of you in different ways to lead me to LAMPS. Thanks for the friendship, laughter, and edification.

My church family, thanks for being a place of healing, love, and encouragement.

Finally, to my fellow LAMPS sisters, and the contributors to this book. Thanks for working with me, and for your fortitude in sharing your heartfelt stories.

Amber Nicole McKinzy

Editor, LAMPS Ministries

Preface

Some opportunities can only be described as God-ordained. It appears at times that life's circumstances will destroy you and inhibit or prevent the fulfillment of your God-given callings and talents. It is amazing that, to the contrary, God uses what the enemy meant for evil, for the good of yourself and others.

My life's circumstances brought me to a place of brokenness, but God led me to LAMPS through a journey of healing and wholeness. As it proclaims in Isaiah 61:3, "To appoint unto them that mourn in Zion, to give unto them beauty for ashes, the oil of joy for mourning, the garment of praise for the spirit of heaviness; that they might be called trees of righteousness, the planting of the LORD, that He might be glorified." How beautiful it is to behold what the Lord brings forth from the ashes!

LAMPS is an acronym for Ladies Abused Mentally, Physically, Sexually, Substance, Self, and Spiritually. This book is a compilation of the testimonies of women who have experienced great transformation through the LAMPS ministry, founded by Rev. Kathy McManus Corson. She has desired the recording of these testimonies to advance the message that there is hope of restoration.

Special thanks go to Sis. Cathy Talent, who helped shoulder the burden for the fruition of this project on Sis. Corson's behalf and felt a strong impression to ask me if I had an interest in writing. She had no way of knowing of my lifelong love and calling to write.

LAMPS has dramatically impacted my life, and I earnestly desire to see other women made whole, so I could not imagine a worthier project to be involved in. It has been one of the greatest honors of my life to compile and edit these redemptive stories.

It has taken great courage for these women to permit their deepest hurts and most painful life experiences to be featured in this manner. Many victims are blamed for their predicament, stigmatized, or accused of creating a false narrative.

Each personal story is a testament to the Word and the Spirit's specified ministrations to provide healing and wholeness. The prayer of every contributor and everyone involved in LAMPS is that this book conveys the message that God's will is that you are made whole in body, soul, and spirit.

Sadly, in many instances in the Body of Christ, attention is placed on physical healing, while the focus on mental, emotional, and spiritual healing is widely neglected. This book truly stands as a witness that God is concerned about the whole person and desires to minister intricately to every aspect of who we are.

Each contributor beautifully highlights unique aspects of how they have been ministered to through LAMPS, thereby developing a well-rounded introduction to its efficacy.

I have been deeply moved as I have worked on polishing each of these stories, and in writing my own. It has all been a part of my journey of healing, as well as a learning experience. I am deeply humbled and highly honored to be a part of seeing this dream of Sis. Corson's come to pass.

Her compassionate and healing spirit is drawn to the wounded. The purpose of this book is to highlight ISSUES, not specific people that perpetrated the hurt. For that reason, each testimony will be accompanied by initials only, and some have been changed for complete anonymity.

There are many even in the church that need to know that they are not alone. The shame and stigma needs to be removed, so that the hurting can be vulnerable and receive healing. Ignoring the past doesn't erase the damage that it caused, but rather causes hardness or callousness to develop in our emotions and spirit.

If we desire to experience revival in our families, communities, churches, and world, we need to first experience it in our own lives. We are greatly hindered in our relationship with God and others when impurities, bitterness, grudges or a lack of forgiveness is present in our hearts. God doesn't want us to live in the past, but He does want us to deal with it and release it.

Jesus urgently desires to not only make you whole, but he longs to send you forth as another mouthpiece of his gracious renewal of abundant life, no longer as a VICTIM, but as a VICTOR!

Amber Nicole McKinzy
Editor, LAMPS Ministries

Foreword

In your lifetime, you will meet many people who will impact and help mold your world. The Rev. Kathy McManus Corson has been and still is one of those individuals for me. Her walk with God has been consistent from youth, and her ongoing commitment to reaching lost souls has been unrelenting.

Her dynamic teachings and preaching have been and are inspiring and transformational! Now, the LAMPS ministry has a far-reaching impact. It was birthed for the broken to be restored and for the attainment of their fullest potential!

As a dynamic "Woman of the Word," her keen insight establishes the foundation for this timely and unprecedented ministry to reach the nations! The Word is without boundaries or restraint!

LAMPS is a ministry founded on hope beyond the breaking! Isaiah 42:3 says, "A bruised reed shall He not break, and the smoking flax shall He not quench: He SHALL bring forth judgment unto truth." Let God have the broken pieces of your life and stand back in amazement at the masterpiece He creates!

The brokenness is not the end; it is a place for the "new" to begin. Isaiah 43:19 states, "Behold, I will do a new thing; now it shall spring forth; shall ye not know it? I will even make a way in the wilderness, and rivers in the desert."

These compiled testimonies are a witness of God's power to bring light to your darkness, that you may escape the gloom and enter the fullness of God's promises!

Psalm 119:105 says, "Thy word is a LAMP unto my feet, and a light unto my path." Our Lord and Savior, Jesus Christ, is a voice for the victims! He is your justifier, your vindicator!

Isaiah 50:8 says, "He is near that justifieth me; who will contend with me? let us stand together: who is mine adversary? let him come near to me." Jesus will stand WITH you and FOR you! And Romans 8:31 states that "if God be for us, who can be against us?"

The LAMPS ministry will guide you in your journey to wholeness. Read this book prayerfully and carefully. Open your heart to the unfathomable possibilities Jesus Christ has for you, the reader. Be blessed, and be changed!

Rev. Sylvia McDaniel
Founder, Inner Circle Ministries

Introduction

LAMPS is a step-by-step healing and deliverance ministry, a journey from hurt to healing, wholeness, and finally helping others heal. We are overcomers by the Blood of the Lamb and the word of our testimony! Only God can make us whole.

In this book, you have the opportunity to experience a supernatural move of God that has enabled each person to continue their journey on the road to wholeness. I believe it will ignite faith for each of you to experience your unique journey of becoming complete and whole.

Every journey starts with one step. Today, my prayer is that you will initiate your story of healing with this book of testimonies. Initially, each individual suffered emptiness in their soul and spirit, but God administered His Word, so, as stated in Colossians 2:10, they could become "complete in Him."

Allow YOUR story to become HIS story! I admonish you to give Him all of your broken pieces, and He can restore you better than new.

It is essential to begin your journey of wholeness by putting first things first, and here are some keys to help you. You must surrender your all to God and allow Him to sit on the throne of your life.

Develop a relationship with God through prayer and His Word. Listen to Him when He speaks to you.

Matthew 6:33 says, "But seek ye first the kingdom of God, and his righteousness; and all these things shall be added unto you."

In Matthew 16:15-20 we read:

> He saith unto them, But whom say ye that I am? And Simon Peter answered and said, Thou art the Christ, the Son of the living God. And Jesus answered and said unto him, Blessed art thou, Simon Barjona: for flesh and blood hath not revealed it unto thee, but my Father which is in heaven. And I say also unto thee, That thou art Peter, and upon this rock I will build my church; and the gates of hell shall not prevail against it. And I will give unto thee the keys of the kingdom of heaven: and whatsoever thou shalt bind on earth shall be bound in heaven: and whatsoever thou shalt loose on earth shall be loosed in heaven. Then charged he his disciples that they should tell no man that he was Jesus the Christ.

Peter had to have a revelation of who Jesus was, in order to discover his own identity. Turn to Jesus, the source of your life, and receive your identity and destiny from Him. Don't allow others to label you. It isn't what others say about you that matters, but your Creator, Jesus.

In Luke 24:49, after the death, burial, and resurrection of Jesus Christ, he told them to go to Jerusalem and tarry until they were endued with power from on high.

The four gospels were written accounts of the life and miracles of the Lord Jesus. The Book of Acts were the actions of the apostles after Jesus ascended into Heaven.

Peter preached the plan of salvation that Jesus had given him the keys to. Acts 2:37 states, "Now when they heard this, they were pricked in their hearts, and said unto Peter and to the rest of the apostles, Men and brethren, what shall we do?"

The response in verse 38 is, "Then Peter said unto them, Repent, and be baptized every one of you in the name of Jesus Christ for the remission of sins, and ye shall receive the gift of the Holy Ghost."

If you have faith in the Lord and want to be made whole:

1. Repent of your sins.

2. Be baptized in Jesus' name.

3. Receive the gift of the Holy Ghost.

4. Find a church that believes and practices the whole gospel.

Romans 14:17 declares, "For the kingdom of God is not meat and drink; but righteousness, peace, and joy in the Holy Ghost."

As the song says, "What can wash away my sins? Nothing but the blood of Jesus. What can make me whole again? Nothing but the blood of Jesus."

I pray that you will find healing, wholeness, and answers in the center of God's will. Jesus loves you, and so do I.

If we can be of help or service to you, please do not hesitate to contact us. May God richly bless and keep you in all you do and everywhere you go.

My prayer for everyone that reads this book is that you will find healing, hope, freedom, deliverance, salvation, help, and direction for your life. I pray that the peace of God will fill your heart and mind. Be made whole in Jesus' name!

Pray 1 Thessalonians 5:23-24, and insert your name: "And the very God of peace sanctify you wholly, and I pray God your WHOLE spirit and soul and body be preserved blameless unto the coming of our Lord Jesus Christ. Faithful is He that called you, who also will do it."

YOUR STORY can become HIS STORY because He is the author and finisher of your faith!

Rev. Kathy McManus Corson

Founder, LAMPS Ministries

Chapter 1 by B.D.M.

God's Art Piece

My testimony doesn't at all take away from the concept that God is still mending and reshaping me and the broken pieces of my life, but I don't want to miss the chance to give God the praise and blessing those He uses in making me what He has designed me to be.

I have heard and tried to practice the scripture for many years. I love God's Word and strive to live it daily. However, I also carry the guilt of not always fully trusting God with my thoughts and actions.

The Lord brought before me the chance to get to know a group of women called "Inner Circle" at a Ladies Ministers Conference. This meeting changed my life. Every Inner Circle event revolves around prayer! You pray, or more precisely, pray until you can't pray anymore! I love to pray!

I found a home with ladies that prayed and taught God's truth. A young, unnamed minister said of one of our meetings, "It's just too much; I don't have the strength." But, oh, I love to become one with His Spirit, praising and worshipping Him as we glean from His Word and commune with Him!

Multiple ministries have been born out of Inner Circle, and one of those ministries is LAMPS. Sis. Kathy McManus Corson birthed this healing ministry from her burden for women wounded by their past. I want to address this aspect of my testimony. LAMPS is an acronym for "Ladies Abused Mentally, Physically, Sexually, Substance, Self, and Spiritually."

Yes, somewhere in there is most of us, but how we heal is where the difference is. Sometimes it's in who is ministering to our spiritual health. Our support system! But too often, we cannot find the right person or place or the understanding to step out of the hurt, destruction, abuse, etc.

Oh, most of the time, we are informed of what we need to do and that we need to let go of our painful circumstances, but have NO reliable support or even anyone that truly believes in us or has the time or resources to help.

Healing is a continual process. Receiving information alone is not sufficient. A doctor can give you pills, but not only is it necessary to understand and follow the regimen he prescribes for you, sometimes there are more profound issues that need addressing to be on an authentic journey of healing.

Sis. Corson taught us scripturally at a LAMPS service that we don't always heal without the formation of scars but that we learn to prevail with them. She displayed an example of Kintsugi, the Japanese art form of putting broken pottery pieces back together, with gold filling in the cracks.

This art stems from the idea of embracing flaws and imperfections and creating an even more sturdy and beautiful piece of art. Indeed I have the broken pieces, and God's Word is the purest of gold, so I should be a lovely, valuable piece of art when God completes His work. And there is work involved, daily! I'm learning how to take the lacquerware (scripture) and trust in God (technique), but I also have to learn how to use the paintbrush of life to varnish the broken surfaces and sprinkle with God's gold.

I've always loved the Word of God, but with my learning disabilities, I couldn't mentally retain it. Now, I find ways to reinforce the scripture so more than just knowing it in my heart, I can speak it from my mind. I don't only apply the Word to myself with guilt and helplessness, but I find it achievable. I'm working on putting myself down less, although I'm struggling in that area.

I don't back down and give up as readily now, but trust that God will lead me through this. If my vision gets dim (and it does), I trust God to shine His light on it or renew it. When I get weary and can't pray like at other times, I don't give up, but I redirect my mind and words. I also don't feel as guilty when others get upset or feel responsible for what goes wrong.

As you can see, brought on from the mental abuse growing up and then picked up by others, I was a mess of hurt and guilt. But no one knew until I was grown and had children that I had been abused (and then only a few), and had a speech impediment and couldn't memorize.

I was ashamed of my identity, so I put on a facade and pretended I already was what I wanted to be. The later abuse got so harsh I couldn't fake it anymore, and my own family thought I was crazy.

Thank God for LAMPS and the words of healing that Sis. Corson revealed for me to use in my brokenness. She has encouraged us that it is okay to be in a state of brokenness but that the vessel shouldn't be discarded. Each one is worth saving and restoring. Allow the scriptures to be the adhesive that puts you back together, and the peace of God will be the gold that shines forth.

When others can see God's mantle on the broken pieces and the beauty of God's love as it mends, it will cause them to recognize and hunger after the undeniable miracle of love!

Am I completely whole? Surely not. I still have to use the paintbrush heavily most of the time, but He is still working on me. I am still experiencing growth.

I may not ever be what God initially wanted me to be, but He still has plans for me. I will not only persevere, but I will be an EXQUISITE ART PIECE that will be a testimony of the creative, marvelous, mending work that He has done in my life.

Chapter 2 by C.P.

A Covering of Grace

I am highly honored to share my testimony, but I must admit that I have significantly struggled in getting started. I want to say "Thank you" for taking the time to read my story.

For this book's purpose, I will share specific abuses and situations that wounded me and left me needing to be healed and made whole. I've experienced many extraordinary yet horrible circumstances that are horrendously difficult to share.

As I share a portion of my experiences with you, I hope that what impacts you the most isn't the pain or brokenness of my story but the grace, mercy, and love of God that rescued, healed, and redeemed my lost soul.

Familial dysfunction was at the root of the earliest memories of the abuse I suffered, curses inherited from previous generations. Enduring unbroken cycles of abuse, feelings of desperate anxiety, fear, confusion, and guilt tormented me. I never knew when the next frenzy of uncontrolled anger, rage, and violence was going to erupt. I never understood why this was happening or what I had done to deserve this treatment.

While I was never directly 'abused' by any of our household members, the side-effects of their problems and confrontations affected my mental and emotional state dramatically. As a small child, I did not know how to identify, understand, or process the circumstances around me.

I learned at a very young age to keep quiet and to myself. In our household, children weren't allowed to have an opinion or vocalize their feelings if it differed from the adult authorities.

Growing up, I was unfamiliar with generational curses, and I couldn't identify what plagued our family, but I realized that our issues were abnormal. I recall instances when an overwhelming terror would grip me. I would get the impression that something or someone was watching me, but no one was ever there. I didn't know how to classify this feeling, and I never spoke out due to the correlating, debilitating fear.

One night in particular, while lying in bed, I became numb with trepidation. It was the kind of fear that takes your breath and causes your heart to race wildly within your chest. I closed my eyes as tightly as I could, hoping not to see anything. When I opened my eyes, I saw a lion crouching and pacing the floor. It was stalking me as though I were its prey, looking for an opportunity to attack.

I realize this may not seem worth mentioning but imagine being a three or four-year-old child and seeing this in the room with you. I was terrified. I did not understand what it meant. Undoubtedly, if I had told anyone, I would've been scolded and sent back to bed, dismissed while being informed of my 'vivid imagination,' or it even being thought that I had a mental illness. I was too afraid to tell anyone, so I buried it in my mind and stayed silent.

I didn't know what it meant then, but I know now that the scripture says in 1 Peter 5:8, "Be sober, be vigilant; because your adversary the devil, as a roaring lion, walketh about, seeking whom he may devour."

Satan had an evil agenda for my life even as a child; he desired to destroy my soul and the plan that God had for my life.

I also suffered sexual abuse. My first memory of it occurred at a distant relative's home. This abuse wasn't from an adult but an older child. He was old enough to know it was wrong but possibly not old enough to fully understand his actions.

It happened to me at such an early age that I didn't comprehend its meaning or impact. I knew it was a secret, and I would be in trouble if I told, so I stayed quiet.

In hindsight, and now that I understand his home's environment, I believe that he mimicked sexual behaviors he witnessed an adult family member performing on his siblings (touching, rubbing, inappropriate body gestures, and body to body contact). These may seem like 'minor' offenses, but they are still damaging and abusive and emotionally, mentally, and spiritually harmful to both parties involved.

I had several other encounters with sexual abuse throughout my early childhood, all committed by an older child, not an adult. Either way, the feelings of shame, guilt, worthlessness, and fear still accompanied the abuse, regardless of who the perpetrator was. These experiences resulted in many future hardships with intimacy, trust, and relationships.

Sometime after this, my parents began to go to church and make lifestyle changes, which thankfully removed me from homes and circumstances that provided the opportunity for further sexual abuse.

Troubling engagements within the spiritual realm became a constant experience for me and grew even darker and more intense after my parents devoted their lives to God. At times I had spiritual encounters in my dreams. These dreams were often so vivid that whatever I experienced in the dream, I could feel physically after waking. I never told anyone, however, because I doubted anyone would believe me.

Satan insidiously keeps us silent through paralyzing fear. I kept my silence for years. I knew the incidents were real and didn't want others to believe that I was crazy.

As an adult, I was smart, successful, and hardworking. People thought and spoke admirably of me. From outward appearances, all appeared to be okay. I went through the motions, going to church, singing the songs, reading God's Word. I prayed, cried, went to youth services and prayer meetings. I involved myself in almost every ministry of the church. I was a faithful, dedicated young saint.

I gave every effort to be tenacious and remain faithful to my upbringing. Emotionally, on the other hand, I fought to endure. I was wounded and confused. I felt like I was an empty wreck. I had no concept of who I was. I didn't realize that I had value and worth. People tell you that you do, but you don't accept it because they don't know the "real you," even though it's true.

I loved God and desperately wanted to please Him, but the burden I carried was too cumbersome for me to bear. The facade I wore to hide the damage began to fade. I couldn't imagine the people who expected so much of me knowing the secrets I held. I didn't know how to surrender, so I fled.

I sought to run as far and as fast as I could from God. He was the only one that knew everything about me, and I was humiliated. At this time, I felt pursued by all of my past traumas, but they came with allies. New friends and a husband came with cigarettes, alcohol, partying, clubs, cocaine, ecstasy, marijuana, methamphetamines, pharmaceutical drugs, rape, and mental, emotional, and physical abuse.

I then entered a cycle of substance abuse, which also comes with cohorts. Substance abuse is usually a frantic effort used in learning to cope and function while dealing with past and present adversity.

Substance abuse opened a 'gateway' or 'portal' for demonic spiritual encounters, attacks, and spiritual activity that I had never experienced before.

One night, in particular, my husband and I went to a friend's house to party. We laughed and drank and smoked. We were having "fun," just a typical night of partying, nothing extraordinary.

Later in the evening, we became increasingly under the influence of drugs, and I experienced a new but unusual occurrence. I progressively lost control of my body. I no longer possessed the necessary motor skills. I became physically paralyzed, and I fell backward onto the sofa. I could not speak or move any part of my body. While lying on the couch, my thoughts were all I could control, and horror began to consume me.

"Am I dying?" I anxiously questioned. "Is this what it feels like to overdose? Do people during an overdose know that they are dying?"

By this time, my sight was no longer in the physical realm. I could see my body lying on the sofa as if I were standing in front of myself. I fully believe my spirit had left my body and that I was in a transition from life to death. I knew at this moment that I was going to die. I began to plead with God and beg Him for mercy.

"Oh God, please don't let me die in this manner! What will my parents think? If I die like this, it will destroy them! I know too much to be in this situation! Please help me! For my parents' sake, please don't let me die from an overdose in a drug house! I promise I will return to you one day! Please!"

At some point, through this mental (or spiritual) pleading, God had mercy on me. The next thing I recall is being back in my body and sitting up on the sofa. God was merciful, and yet I did not return to Him for several years.

I lived through a few more years of drug use. During this time, my marriage became a hostile, abusive, living hell. Another cycle of everything I had suffered through as a child began again, but this time it was more intense and destructive. It manifested itself differently, but it was the same abuse.

My ex-husband became extremely abusive. He was cunning and passive-aggressive. He would manipulate situations and words to make it appear as though he loved and cared for me but had no problem physically or sexually abusing me. The good times were great, but the bad times were horrible. When it all began to fall apart, it was always my fault. There was no in-between.

In this marriage, I became so afraid for my life that marijuana and alcohol no longer soothed or pacified the anxiety and fear that tormented me. The devastating awareness of death hovered over me for months. It gripped every part of my individuality. I did not know who would take my life or how it would come to pass, but I knew I was doomed.

This obsession with death convinced me that sleep was unsafe. I was terrified even to lie down and close my eyes. I could not defend myself if I were unconscious of knowing when danger was imminent. I felt as though I had a bulls-eye on my back, and it was only a matter of time before someone took me out.

During this time, cocaine and methamphetamines became a regular part of my life. It allowed me to stay up for five, six, or even seven days straight. Consider that these drugs presented a host of sickening situations that I will not mention, but the terms "slum" and "scum" sum it up accurately. My life was similar to a cesspool of sewage, and I was drowning in it.

The excessive drug use eventually came to an end, but not before an intense encounter with a demonic spirit. The night of the episode, I had just completed a five or six-day meth binge. I was so physically and mentally exhausted I knew I had to 'come down' and sleep.

I finally convinced myself it would be okay to sleep just a few hours. I got into bed and laid there wide-eyed in the dark for a while, fighting the thought of not ever waking up. Yet, I was so physically exhausted I knew I could not go without sleep any longer. After a while, I decided to close my eyes.

As soon as I did, that petrifying terror of someone watching me took hold of me. I knew something was standing over me. I opened my eyes, hoping nothing was there.

Immediately, I saw a black figure in the shape of a man, which reached down and grabbed me around my throat. It instantly began to strangle me, and I tried to scream. I attempted to kick or hit my husband to wake him, but I couldn't move. I was completely incapacitated.

The demonic spirit began to speak to me. It kept repeating, "You ran away from God, and you don't have the power to stop me. There isn't anything you can do, and you are going to die."

I couldn't move nor speak. I could only lie there and cry. I remember feeling hot, wet tears roll down the sides of my face and into my hair.

I hopelessly tried to speak out against it, but I was helpless. Right at that moment, gasping for my next breath, I realized I had control of one thing-my mind. The evil spirit could control my body, but he did not have the authority to control my mind!

He stated the truth when he said that I left God and had no power, but what he said was a half-truth. I had walked away from God, but HE had NEVER walked away from me!

I began to meditate on the name of Jesus and tried to speak it out. "Jesus, Jesus." The third time I tried to speak the name of Jesus, it flowed out of my mouth and into the atmosphere!

I instantly experienced freedom, and the spirit vanished!

The fear, shock, and sheer terror did not leave with that spirit, however. Even though I escaped the angel of death a second time, I was so held captive by my past that it would still be years before I turned back to God.

God has been abundantly merciful to me, and I will never, ever be able to repay Him or express how tremendously thankful I am to Him! He has rescued me time after time! I know the prayers of my family, friends, and church protected me and kept me within the covering of God's grace.

I've shared all of this not for pity but for God to receive glory through my story! If God loves ME enough to bring me through all of these things and more, imagine what He can do for YOU!

LAMPS has been a vital part of my recovery since coming back to God. I have attended 12 step meetings and spoken with people about my struggles caused by my past.

While they are well intended and can offer some good advice, what I received in those meetings were helpful but not healing.

Through the LAMPS ministry, I've come to know that only God can heal a wounded soul. Self-help will only get you so far, but God's help is boundless and unconditional! The prayers, preaching of the Word, and ministry of Sis. Kathy Corson has encouraged me time after time.

Because of her commitment, dedication, and obedience to God, I have been able to surrender, forgive, heal, and be transformed into what God has called me to be. I may not be perfect, but I am conforming to who God designed me to be!

Having a support system that will expound God's truth to you, even when it's convicting and not easy to hear, is precisely necessary for recovery. LAMPS has most definitely established that guideline for me!

Recovery is difficult at times, but when we become resolute and have the right encouragement, anything is possible!

Proverbs 27:6 says, "Faithful are the wounds of a friend; but the kisses of an enemy are deceitful." I thank God for the people He has placed in my life who will tell me the truth!

LAMPS is a network of women that have decided to no longer be victims held prisoners of their past but who have chosen to rise and become victors! We are an army of beautifully broken sisters equipped with prayer and the Word of God, reaching out to those that are broken and feel alone. His Word is a LAMP!

Psalm 119:105 states, "Thy word is a lamp unto my feet, and a light unto my path." You are not alone! He will never leave or forsake you!

In Isaiah 42:16 God says, "And I will bring the blind by a way that they knew not; I will lead them in paths that they have not known: I will make darkness light before them, and crooked things straight. These things will I do unto them, and not forsake them."

We need each other to recover! We need God to give us a sound mind through the Holy Ghost to instruct and guide us!

"For God hath not given us the spirit of fear; but of power, and of love, and of a sound mind." (2 Timothy 1:7)

We need to forgive to be free. Forgiveness is the key that unlocks our hearts and allows God to come in and start the process of healing and restoration. "But if ye forgive not men their trespasses, neither will your Father forgive your trespasses." (Matthew 6:15)

I have learned that forgiving someone doesn't necessarily do anything for the other person, but it frees us completely! Forgiveness is not a feeling, but it's a choice. It's a choice that will restore life!

We can do all things through Christ, but we must let Him in! Invite Him into your heart, mind, spirit, and life, and He will free you from your past if you surrender to Him wholeheartedly!

Again, I would like to say "Thank you." Thank you for taking the time to read a portion of "My Story." Thank you to Sis. Kathy Corson for being a willing vessel of God's glory. Thank you to all the women who have bravely come forward to share their stories with all who will take the time to read them!

Thank you to all those who have been instrumental in helping me reach this place of recovery in my life. I will continue to heal and strengthen with my LAMPS sisters fighting the good fight with me.

And remember, when you look into the face of a stranger, they have a story, as well. Bravely and proudly show your scars! They could open a lifeline for other ladies in tragic need of being rescued, and to find the courage to speak out! Go forward in Jesus' Name!

Chapter 3 by M.M.

Through the Fire

My journey began three years ago. I was walking through darkness. I felt alone and needed God to intervene in areas that I didn't share with anyone. I had no mentors, spiritual guidance, or encouragement. I had a foundation in the church. I knew the power of prayer and the miracles that God had performed in my life.

I attended my first LAMPS service on November 3, 2017, in Webster, TX. I had been invited to the LAMPS services before, but I wasn't ready to face the spiritual giants of my past until I got an invitation on October 31, 2017, to come and support a friend. That's the only reason why I went.

I had received an invitation before, but it hadn't yet been the right time. God has since revealed to me that He operates in certain times and seasons.

I found it hard to trust in myself and others. In prayer and fasting, I opened up my heart, mind, and spirit to the call of God to be used out of my comfort zone.

After facing myself and my fears, the Lord began to reveal issues in my heart and life. I needed to forgive myself, God, and others, that I had been unable to forgive before.

Being a part of the LAMPS ministry, I had the opportunity to meet many wonderful women that God ordained to speak into my life. Even before my situation fully manifested, I had no concept or ability to foretell how my life would unfold. God told me that I would be stunned by my future.

Until now, I have witnessed things transpire through trusting in God because I was unable to trust in man. This lack of trust, prayer life, or walk with God caused me to live in a place of spiritual darkness. I was an empty shell, falling short of living for God in the manner that I knew how.

My husband worked a lot. I would go to church and come home, but I wanted to throw in the towel. There was a point that I didn't want to go back to church because my husband wasn't there, and I knew we weren't living according to God's will.

My husband worked a tremendous amount, and while he wasn't living a completely ungodly lifestyle, he wasn't entirely giving God his all. My kids didn't have the example they needed.

My husband was overworked, and his schedule was the first area in which God intervened. The Lord told us that mountains would move and that we would be awed by His works.

My husband had been working shift work since he was 19, for the first 23 years of our marriage. He was able to get off shift work and began working straight days, with no more nights.

For years, I had asked God to change his schedule because I desired to submit to my husband as a man of God. He started going to church, and I didn't have to come home and share what transpired in the services, but it was when I started going to LAMPS that he began to see a tremendous change in me.

I was spiritually nourished and encouraged by loving and caring people. I had never seen this level of ministry before, with ladies like Sis. Kathy Corson and Sis. Cathy Talent. They offered generous encouragement and extraordinarily expounded the Word.

When we began to grow and transform spiritually and adjust our lifestyles, praying and fasting together, going to church, and becoming involved, God started manifesting Himself and told us that He would use us out of our comfort zones. God said that He would perform in our lives in specific ways in the future and that we needed to trust Him.

I started losing my hair two years ago. I remember thinking that it was Alopecia. I started getting spots, and my hair started falling out the day before we began to pack and get ready to go to North American Youth Congress (NAYC) of 2019.

I told my husband that I didn't want to go and to take the kids without me. However, he strongly encouraged me to go. For four months prior, we had been feeling drawn to attend NAYC with our kids. We didn't understand the purpose, but while we were there, I received a prophecy that God would heal the cause of my hair loss.

That Thursday night, I went to hear Jack Cunningham preach at the NAYC healing service. I had never experienced God's touch as powerfully as I did in this service. It felt like electricity moving from the nape of my neck up to the crown of my head.

I shielded myself and ducked down because it greatly frightened me. I didn't comprehend what was taking place or what was happening to my body. I went into a state of shock. My husband asked if I was okay, and I tried to explain the experience I had had, but he said that God had touched and healed me.

With the spirit of worship that God had given me, I began to worship until I was too weak to continue. Within a month after coming home, I lost the rest of my hair and became completely bald.

During that time, in prayer, God gave me many revelations and shared much wisdom from the Book of Job. People have believed me to be crazy, and many have thought I had done something wrong and that my hair loss resulted from God's judgment.

However, God kept speaking. I kept going to LAMPS and Inner Circle, which has all been a massive part of my life, and I became ever closer to the ladies involved. God put me right in the center of it. God has been manifesting Himself to me in innumerable ways, and it has been an unspeakable joy.

I am very humbled that God would be able to use someone like me, but he uses the broken. I am now allowing His Spirit to operate, and I am fully trusting in Him. He has also found confidence in me and helps me live a holy life, bear the fruit of the Spirit, and walk in the full armor of God.

It is of utmost importance to put on the full armor of God daily and to die out to our flesh. It's not always easy, but He never promised that it would be. He did, however, promise a peace that passes all understanding, which is one of the most remarkable gifts that I have received from God. He had given me the word "revelation," and He revealed not only who I am in God, but who He is.

It makes me heartsick to admit because I was brought up in church, but I never had the revelation of who God was. I now have a full understanding of it, and I am walking in its truth. I am now joyful, and I can share my testimony, whereas before, I wouldn't talk to people.

I didn't have the confidence to speak up previously, but God has afforded me spiritual boldness, authority, and power in that area, as the Word intended. God called us to be apostles, to freely share the power and wonder of our God, and to win others to Jesus Christ.

So many of our loved ones do not have to be lost, but we have to go out in the world and share the Good News. We must compel them to come, no matter what they think of us. Job's friends thought he was crazy and condemned him. He also found himself in a pile of ash, scraping the boils off his skin once God allowed Satan to touch him physically.

If Satan could have killed him, he would have, but God allowed him to destroy all that Job had because God knew He could trust him. God allowed the devil to destroy his health. My health has been affected as well, but this is the devil's last-ditch effort. He has no power over me.

His attacks have caused me to have a more profound passion in my pursuit and service to God. Doctors have shared their opinions, but I won't go back to them because of what God has spoken to me. God has proclaimed His healing over me, and in His timing, the fulfillment is going to be fantastic and exciting. My miracle will be manifest at a time for Him to receive the most glory.

I told Him that I didn't want my old garment of self back, and I don't want my old hair back. I yearn for better things that God has for me. Not everyone will believe, but that doesn't concern me. I am thankful to God for the people who will come to salvation by seeing my hair grow back. God has given people visions, dreams, and prophecies that my hair is coming back.

One of the most compelling prophecies that I have received is that God has placed me in a cocoon and that when He finishes, I will be the most beautiful that I have ever been in my life. He said that He starts from the inside, and then He works on the outside. It is humbling that God would even acknowledge me.

When I first attended LAMPS, I didn't know Sis. Corson or any of the other ladies, but they have spoken into my life. Every service has been more profound, like stepping into new dimensions.

One prophecy that I received was that God was suiting me up and putting me on the battlefield, that I was going to stand and fight, as in worship. I love to worship, and being a worshipper has become my identity. That was the purpose of my creation.

I love seeing people receive the Holy Ghost. I am more excited than I have ever been about witnessing to people, and being bald draws others to me. When people see me, they believe I'm dying and either want to pray for me or show sympathy, but when I tell them how God has been working, they walk away changed. They walk away with a newfound understanding and feeling.

We may not recognize our spiritual impact, but when we sow the seed like God has commanded us to do, we have to realize that we're not responsible for the increase.

I am confident that there will be a great harvest, and I feel strongly in my spirit that God will allow me to witness it soon. I have family, friends, community, and neighbors that need salvation, and if it takes me being without hair so that people are more willing or comfortable to talk to me now than they were before, then so be it.

Perhaps God has allowed me to go through this just so that I have the memory and testimony. My children are also miracles, because I was unable to have children. I have a marriage that many people aren't blessed to have. Even if this ends in death, I will trust Him no matter what. I know, though, without a shadow of a doubt, that when I do pass, that I will meet the one who transformed me forever.

My spiritual eyes are now open. My perception has changed, and it started with LAMPS. Amazingly, it started with me going to support a friend because my nature is to help and to love people.

The Spirit of God saturated me so entirely that I could not contain myself. I sat there while tears ran down my face, and I was perplexed by the experience. I was eager to meet everyone and find out more about them. It has been mind-blowing to know Sis. Corson, and the other women.

I had asked God to send me someone, even if it was just one person. We need mentors and people to invest their time, wisdom, and walk with God with us. It is so essential. It's unifying, and unity brings power. God's in the midst of two or three that will agree together. I love LAMPS; it has a very significant role to play in God's Kingdom.

I have not only learned to trust, but God has taught me to discern spirits, and specifically the demonic spirits that I was battling. I had been fighting the spirit of control. I wasn't controlling, but I had allowed other people outside of my marriage to govern me. My thinking patterns, decisions, and actions were all restricted by this spirit of manipulation.

I didn't realize its control until God revealed to me in prayer that I was under its influence and that I needed to sever ties with those who were having this effect on me. He told me that I was not a child and that as an adult, allowing this control was not the same thing as showing respect. He revealed that my submission was to God and my husband and that a Jezebel spirit was in control of me.

I had also been dealing with fear. These forces dominated my walk with God and kept me from being close to Him because those things are not of God. It is not God's will to be under the control of spirits that others are dealing with or under the thumb of their opinions.

If Job had taken other's incorrect opinions upon himself, God wouldn't have used him as an example to Satan, and his story wouldn't be in the Word of God.

I've asked God for the ability to discern these spirits. You can't slay the giant unless you can see what and who he is. You have to know what you're fighting, and you find that out in prayer and fasting. You have to strive to live for the Lord. If you draw near unto Him, He will doubtlessly draw near unto you.

God ordained that I would be a part of LAMPS and that I would be offered love and encouragement by women that didn't even know me.

I didn't feel worthy, but they beautifully taught me the meaning of Leviticus 19:34: "But the stranger that dwelleth with you shall be unto you as one born among you, and thou shalt love him as thyself; for ye were strangers in the land of Egypt: I am the Lord your God."

One of the prophecies that I received at a LAMPS conference brought me to this scripture. A woman was prophesying over me, and in the manner she was praying, I thought God was calling me to the foreign mission field. She told me that I would go and "speak and tell."

She said that I would go and speak in a land that wasn't my land. My husband works here in the states, and our lives and our children's lives are based here, but I wondered if God would take me to a mission field in another place.

I began to question myself if I would be willing to pack up and go, and I told the Lord that He would have to speak to my husband first so that we could all go.

I have been around family and others that have not received me. I've lost relationships, but when you know that you have heard the voice of God, and you know God is leading you, and you trust Him with your whole heart, then nothing else matters.

You know that even when you're not worthy or faithful, that God is always faithful. I have seen that come to pass, and I know that I am not alone. He is continually giving me more of himself: His love, His touch, and His Spirit.

You have to go through the fire. You can't teach something that you haven't learned yourself. I thank God for this revelation and for learning the purpose of seasons. I've repented for wasting so many years of my life and not wholeheartedly living for God or sincerely knowing Him.

However, He said that I am like a tree planted by the rivers of water and that I would be fruitful in my season. I told Him that I desired deeply planted roots, and part of that foundation came by being raised in the truth, but God said that He didn't condemn me and that He would bring beauty from the ashes.

Everyone's seasons change from time to time. We each have to go through situations to learn to rely on God's presence and perfect timing. God sees and understands our hearts, regardless of our limitations.

He knows when and how to perform His will and how to get us to focus on Him alone. It was my time. He has transformed, restored, and renewed my life through LAMPS, divinely designed by God to birth life-changing and miraculous moments.

A Woman After God's Heart

Before I begin my story, I take responsibility for my bad decisions. I realize many of these things would not have happened if I had been obedient and more in tune with God. Here is my testimony.

I grew up in a dysfunctional family. My parents genuinely loved me, but my dad was verbally and physically abusive. He backslid when I was eight years old. Although my oldest sibling received the most abuse, we all experienced his wrath. By the time I was 19, I was desperate to escape. All my friends were getting married, so it seemed fitting.

One day I met a man while visiting a new church with my mom. He gave me the creeps, and I held no attraction for him. I couldn't understand why, but I felt unnerved around him. He eventually began to invite me to the mall at different times to help him shop for outings.

I was appalled at the thought of going on a date with him, but my dad appeared to like him, so I reasoned that I should give him a chance. He assured me that we were going as friends.

I remember the day we went to the mall, holding on to the car door as if I were going to jump out at a moment's notice. I still can't perceive why I gave him a chance.

We dated a few months before he asked me to marry him. I could not overcome the odd feeling he gave me. He attended church, so I thought my intuition was ludicrous. I also felt that I was too pathetic to have anyone better, so I believed I didn't have much of an option.

All of my friends were either married or had moved away. I cannot explain why I continued to date and marry someone I didn't love, especially concerning the weird impression I got from him! What was I thinking? I was young and feared that no one would ever love me. My looks had often been criticized, and no other options were presenting themselves.

My logic was that if I could survive living with my dad, then I could handle being married to a guy that I simply thought was strange. He was somewhat handsome, after all, and he seemed to say all of the right things.

Even on our wedding day, I thought that if someone asked me about it, I would have said I shouldn't marry him! I would have fled, and he would never have seen me again!

The first couple of months were commonplace. He worked evenings while I worked days, and we shared the weekends. He eventually quit going to church. His attitude became hostile toward me, and I was confident that he was seeing someone else.

Trusting him became more and more difficult. His words and actions frightened me. One night he told me that he brought home something that would make me happy, but he wouldn't allow me to see it. We had dinner and went to bed.

During intimacy that evening, he inserted an unknown object, which I believed to be a knife. Even to this day, I suffer from unbearable pain. When I began to cry and express hurt, he mocked me and shoved the object further inside. "It doesn't hurt! You're a sissy!" When I finally convinced him to stop, I could barely move. I suffered for days afterward.

The situation kept deteriorating. One day he brought home a co-worker that repulsed me. I couldn't even look at him. They stayed in the car, and I couldn't tell what they were doing. I went outside to say hello, but my husband jumped out of the vehicle. He grabbed me and threw me against the wall. He yelled, "Don't ever come out to the car again!" I cannot prove it, but it appeared that they were caressing each other.

One night I discovered him with his boss's wife alone at her apartment. I was too terrified to confront them, unsure of what he would do. I was being threatened and abused, and I tried to hide it. My parents had taught me that you could not abandon your marriage, so I stayed and kept silent.

I eventually (somewhat) confided in my pastor's wife, but she advised me that I was overly emotional. She gave me a book on handling this topic in a troubled marriage. When my husband found the book, I paid dearly for my confession.

My health was in decline. I was becoming sick, gaining weight, and I struggled with frantic emotions and female-related issues. It seemed I was going mad, and my husband had almost convinced me that it was true.

On our last evening together, he informed me that he would be late for work. We planned to have dinner with my parents beforehand. As soon as he got there, he began to call me names and tried to hit me, but my dad grabbed him and kicked him outside.

I took this opportunity to disclose all of the details. My family helped me pack my things the next day, and I moved back home and filed for divorce. For about six months, he stalked me before moving away.

I healed as time progressed but became lonely. My dad's temperament had improved, but life with my parents hadn't gotten much better. I longed for companionship, despite the lack of comfort in my former marriage.

One weekend I met a guy at a singles event at another church. Being with my peer group was appealing, as well as the opportunity to make new friends.

It was a pleasant outing in the country. I met several new people and thoroughly enjoyed their company. I was especially drawn to a tall blonde with blue eyes. We spent the weekend laughing, talking by the fire, and I realized that I was genuinely attracted to him.

He was in the Navy. He requested my phone number and asked me to accompany him when he got on his flight back to the station. His involvement in the Navy intrigued me. I dreamed of being by his side and traversing the world.

I thought that would be our last encounter, but he contacted me the next day. We continued to talk, and a couple of months later, I got on a plane to visit him.

We spent the entire weekend together. At night I stayed with a lady he knew from the local church, and I spent the days with him. Our time together was so romantic, and my attraction for him was so compelling. He proposed, I accepted, and we got married.

I realize now how unwise my decision was, but I was young and alone. I desperately longed for affection, and it clouded my judgment. We were in love, and I felt confident that we could persevere.

We began a life together in a small one-bedroom apartment near the base. Within a couple of weeks, I recognized that I once again faced a miserable plight. He told me that he still loved his ex-girlfriend, and he hoped that I could live up to his expectations. He didn't care for my Pentecostal faith and wanted me to change my manner of dress. He said that I was "lucky" that he had married me because I was a little plump, and he forbade me to gain any additional weight.

I was shattered. Both sides of my family were large, and at 5'5" and 120 pounds, I already had to eat sparingly to be the size I was. I had multiple concerns about our relationship. I slipped into a carnal lifestyle, including alcohol, parties, and worldly clothing. I don't blame all of my decisions on him because I already desired to dress differently. I never intended to go as far as I did. We didn't use drugs, but we were active in the bar scene.

The Navy caused us to move often, but we finally settled in the east. There were many lifestyle differences to adjust to, which added to the stress of my husband's disapproval. I was overwhelmed. I was not allowed to cry in his presence, and the price was profound if I did.

The mistreatment grew worse. One day he lied and told me we were going somewhere. When I discovered it was a lie, I was overwrought. I began to cry and protest his cruelty, so he picked me up and threw me outside. I hit the car parked beside our home, and if it hadn't been there, I would have hit the tree. I know God was protecting me. I should have left him then, but I was more afraid to flee than to stay. He always denied that he meant to harm me, but I'm not sure.

Somehow I still had a lot of resilience. After being married a few months, my husband grabbed me in the swimming pool, held me down, and stood on top of me until I was close to drowning. He did this multiple times. I wouldn't even have the chance to take a deep breath before going underwater. After finally releasing me, he would find it hilarious when I popped back up. I was already fearful of the water, and these experiences increased my terror.

My thoughts were divided. Although I questioned my decision to marry, my husband convinced me that he was the quality partner, and I was causing the turmoil. He had me indoctrinated that I couldn't make it without him, so I strove to change and be what he demanded. I lost my identity.

As many women do, I desired a baby, but it seemed hopeless. I couldn't get pregnant after trying for several months, and I finally found out that I was infertile. The doctor callously gave me the news, but it stung like a knife. I was despondent; I had dreamed of carrying a child in my womb all my life. My spouse assured me that we would adopt.

Time crept on, and my situation grew bleaker. I honestly didn't realize that I was suffering abuse. I ultimately decided that

I was tired of living for the world, and wanted to give my life back to Jesus, but my spouse refused to allow me to go to an Apostolic church. I had visited other churches, trying to find a substitute, but they all seemed empty.

I'm so thankful for a praying mom. I found out later that she had been praying the entire time. I shared with her that I wanted to get back into the church, but it wasn't currently possible. Unfortunately, it would still be a few years.

While my spouse was at work, I snuck out and found a UPC church, but they didn't welcome outsiders. I hoped making changes to my appearance might make a difference, but they still weren't receptive. Some churches would not even speak to me, while others shook my hand as if I had a disease.

If they could only understand that my heart yearned for a welcome touch and an invitation to pray. It never happened. I was treated like a plague, so for a couple more years I decided that church wasn't for me. My hunger for God didn't diminish, however, but nothing else satisfied. I determined that I would live for God and go to a church where I could and worship God to the best of my ability.

One day we had to take the motorcycle because our car was in disrepair, but I had decided I would only wear skirts from then on. He ordered me to go and put on pants, but I shakily stood my ground. I informed him that I was going to obey this teaching.

At first, it seemed that he would accept it because he just got on the bike and drove off. I thought I had gained a great victory, but I hadn't gained any headway at all. After we got back from our errand, he commanded me to get off the bike first. As I positioned myself to climb off, he leaned the scalding pipe into my leg. He swore that it was an accident, but I know that it was purposeful. Two weeks later, he did the same thing again, and I still have the scars.

After my husband got out of the Navy, we moved back to our hometown. I believed that our families being close by could help our marriage to heal. My husband's family was biased and assured me that I was the problem. They insisted that I should go to whatever church he decided and said that our issues were because I was spoiled. I accepted their opinion as truth.

My dad got back in the church. My parents wanted me to leave my spouse permanently and attend their church, but I wanted to go where I felt welcomed. My husband wouldn't attend any of the churches I liked, and he wouldn't allow me to go either.

One evening my mom tried to get me to go with her, but I didn't care for her church, and I knew my spouse wouldn't let me go. She became furious and said, "Well, just burn in hell, then!" I know that she was trying to wake me up, but her words wounded me. I don't believe that is the appropriate way to reach someone.

I was tired of the abuse and told my husband I would leave if we didn't get back in church. I said that I would attempt to please him in my manner of dress but that nothing would stop me from getting back in church.

My husband had an Apostolic family member that invited us to come and help with their church. They lived in a western state, and although there were challenges, the culture was a less complicated adjustment.

I felt confident that the environment would be conducive to overcoming our issues and creating a successful marriage. I still loved him and did not want to face another divorce!

I was so excited! We were starting a new life and going to church together! Even though we had issues that needed resolution, the pastor supported us and taught us how to forgive and live for God! I know the pastor had his hands full with us.

I began to fast and pray, and otherwise make every effort to connect with God. I wanted my marriage to work, and I loved my husband more than anything besides God, but it was no longer the number one priority.

As I drew closer to God, my situation seemed to calm down. The abuse stopped for a time, and we devoted ourselves to church and ministry. We experienced a great few years. Our lives weren't perfect, but I believed that we would be fine.

Over time, he became the youth pastor of our church and appeared to be thriving. He no longer verbally abused me and displayed genuine care for the first time.

I was gaining knowledge of God's attentiveness and how He desires a profound relationship with us. I was growing in my fellowship and communion with Him.

In the evening, we would go to the church and pray, and the time would pass so quickly. My spouse would alert me that it was time to go, and what I thought was just a few minutes was, in fact, much longer. God began to give me revelation, visions, and dreams, and I would wake up speaking in tongues.

My husband's love for the truth and ministry ultimately began to fade, and he resigned as the youth pastor. I was greatly distressed.

I loved working with the kids; they were my world. I somehow managed to pick up the pieces of my shattered heart and continued on.

My health continued to decline, and I finally learned that I had a thyroid issue. I foolishly thought that because there was a reason for my weight issue, he would understand. However, it only made him angrier. He called me many insulting and derogatory words. Like many women, I wrongly believed that I wasn't being abused because he wasn't hitting me.

On the bright side, the situation seemed to improve. Thankfully he wasn't drinking or throwing me around anymore, but his attitude towards me was inconsistent. There would be times he loved me fiercely, and then all of a sudden he would tell me that he didn't love me anymore, and I needed to go home.

I would go home weeping to my parents until he decided he wanted me back. I would be at my parents for about a month, before he would ask me to come back. My dad had finally gotten back in church, and our relationship began to heal.

I cannot prove this part of my story, so I hesitate to share, but I knew I wasn't safe. Unfortunately, I was too naive to heed the warnings. Looking back, I believe he would have killed me if given a chance, and this will be corroborated further in my story.

In one of these instances, he had come to my parents, profusely apologizing and asking me to come home. I consented and packed my things. On our way westward, we stopped at the Grand Canyon. It was my first time there. He began to grill and suggested that I dangle my feet over the rim while eating. He knew I was a daredevil and said that it could give me something to brag about.

It wasn't until years after the marriage dissolved that I realized how close I came to death. When it finally dawned on me, it hit me like a lightning bolt. I can't imagine what I was thinking. He could have so effortlessly pushed me off and claimed that I fell, and there would have been no proof otherwise.

Thankfully God's hand was upon me. Thinking back on his behavior that day, I believe he intended to kill me. While sitting on the edge, he would stand behind me but would refuse to sit beside me when I asked. He also became agitated when others came to the rim next to us. I asked him several times why it mattered, and he said it wasn't as romantic.

I left my husband once again for what I was convinced was the last time. I was broken and weary of the heartache. I was absolutely in love with Jesus, and knew I needed nothing more.

I drove 2000 miles to my parents and got settled in. I found a new job and a caring new church. Life was improving! I didn't consider the influence of his family, including our pastor. My husband asked me to come back, and my pastor told me that I had no right to leave.

It seemed as if I had no choice. I did not want another divorce or to disappoint God. I once again prepared to go back to my husband, knowing the situation I would face. This time I told God that I was going in obedience, and I asked Him to deliver me from evil.

I understand that I contributed to our issues. I dealt with the highs and lows of depression because of my condition, and I could be stubborn and temperamental.

I told him on the way home that I knew that everything would be the same as before. He laughed and said I should not have come back.

Anger began to rise within me, but I kept praying. Over the next couple of years, I grew less trusting of my spouse and even closer to Jesus. My circumstances were rough, but I no longer feared what my spouse would do to me. I told God that I was willing to do whatever it took to be closer to Him. My prayer was that God would make me "a woman after his own heart."

He kept hurling taunts, sneers, and threats, but it no longer tormented me. I even invited him to hit me because I thought it might be my escape. The doctors were eventually able to stabilize my thyroid medications, and I was also diagnosed with Hashimoto AutoImmune Disease. I was starting to feel like my older self again, but I still suffered from terrible pain.

I began to feel hope for us again. After all, if I were the cause of all the issues, then fixing myself would certainly improve our circumstances. If only I could change my looks, personality, and ambitions, then he would love me, right? The problem was, I could only be myself.

I attempted to make the changes he wanted. I became more assertive to win his love. I drove myself beyond my limits and discovered that there were things that I didn't want to alter, and other issues that were out of my control.

I genuinely loved my husband, even though I now don't know why, and I sincerely believed that I was the cause of all the blame.

A couple of years later, he quit going to church, began smoking and became even more difficult to live with. It broke my heart because I knew that God could use us. He was throwing it all away, and I had no control over it.

God warned me in visions of what would happen, but if my spouse would only submit, we would be blessed abundantly. I tried to tell him what God had told me, but he had hardened his heart and wouldn't believe me. God shared with me that it was not my trial but that it would involve me.

One day we took the day off work to take care of some errands. His demeanor and attitude were much worse than usual, and I was furious! We got home that evening and were still sitting in the car. He was screaming that I was such a loser. He finally yelled, "Have you wondered why I'm so mean to you today?" It wasn't easy to hold back from telling him that it wasn't much different than other days. I fought back tears, gritted my teeth, and said, "What?" I assumed I had displeased him somehow, as usual.

However, what he said totally wrecked my world, and I've not been the same since. He growled, "I've been having an affair!"

I sat there in silence for several minutes, unable to speak. I tried to grasp what he was saying, but I couldn't believe it. I had put up with him for 13 years, and he could so casually throw it away. I was so angry I could have killed him. He went into the house, but I stayed in the car, trying to comprehend what he had said.

As I gained my composure and went inside, questions swirled through my mind. Had they been intimate, or was he bluffing? Did he love her? Would he leave me or could we work this out? How long had he been having an affair?

I was barely able to ask him even a couple of questions. I could tell that he didn't care if I left or stayed, but he definitely didn't want me around anymore. I could stay at the house, but he was going to leave. We were through. He was not going to end his relationship with the other woman.

I wasn't financially stable enough to make it on my own, so my next option was to move back to my parents.

I am still horrified by my next thought. I had been sitting on the couch for quite a while, and my husband was in the room. I made up my mind that the best route to take was to kill us both.

I knew the location of the gun. I knew he slept soundly. All I had to do was wait for him to fall asleep. I went into the bedroom to check, but he was still up. I asked him if he were going to bed, but he looked straight at me and said, "I know what you're about to do, and I'm not foolish enough to go to sleep." I was so enraged that I sat on the couch and waited for him to go to sleep.

I'm thankful now that it didn't happen, but I had every intention at the time to kill him and myself. I ended up falling asleep sitting up on the couch, and I awoke the next morning to a bright and sunny day. He had left for work as if nothing had happened. I managed to get dressed and went to work. I found out later that several people had felt impressed to pray for us both, although they didn't know why.

Everything seems to blur from that point. I began to prepare to go back to my parents, but my pastor called and asked to meet with me. He told me once again that he didn't believe I had a right to leave because my husband claimed he hadn't yet been intimate with the other woman. I was in turmoil, mentally and emotionally.

I was supposed to remain with someone who often tells me he doesn't love me, openly rejects me, and has a girlfriend? I left feeling like a loser, devoid of the will to live. I emotionally shut down. My courage was gone.

I went home and told my husband what was said, and he became indignant. I was terrified of what he might do, but I was too weak to care. I would leave for work without money for food and come home to a house with no food. He would take his girlfriend on dates, and he alone had access to our finances, including my checks in the bank. He wouldn't get home until around midnight, while I tried to survive each day.

We had two cars, so I can't remember why I took him to work every morning. It was possibly so I could jealously watch him as he watched her go inside. I despised her. It was hard to contain myself, but I wanted to attack her. I would watch him watch her get out of the car. I would watch her smile at him. Every day I became more calloused inside.

Needing to pass the time and unleash my vicious anger, I would leave his job and go work out. I would then get dressed and would get through my day in a foul mood. I quickly got fired.

One Sunday morning, I awoke and began to get ready for church. It surprised me to see my spouse also getting up. He said the pastor had insisted that he be there. I had a glimmer of hope, reasoning that perhaps God's presence would be so compelling that he would surrender!

There was a visiting minister that morning. His first words were, "I'm supposed to be on the East Coast this morning, but God sent me here to tell someone that this is your day. Either you repent and surrender to me, or you'll never feel my presence again."

I was convinced that the message was to us, probably more to myself than anyone. I repented of everything I could imagine. All of the church people were on their faces. My spouse prayed, which gave me hope. I asked him if he were giving his life back to God. He said he was, but he never apologized to me.

I wasn't initially concerned about the lack of apology. Our marriage needed healing, and I thought his apology would be forthcoming. We had both contributed to damaging our union, but I knew that if we could submit to God that we could recover.

He informed me the next day that he ended the relationship with his girlfriend, and our pastor encouraged marital counseling. Our appointment was at 5:00, but my husband didn't even leave until 6:00, and it was an hour's drive. The counselor was no longer there, and he laid the blame on her and said that she would have been there if she genuinely wanted to save our marriage.

I was vainly holding onto the slightest hope, but it became more apparent that he desired our marriage to end. I loved him despite his actions. I had been taught that whatever the circumstances, you strive to make it work.

A couple of weeks later, our pastor suggested that we take a pleasant vacation to a place like Hawaii, but my husband said he wouldn't splurge like that for me. It was during the holidays, and he promised that we would visit my family for Thanksgiving. I was excited to spend time with both sides of our family.

I brought just a few clothes, a couple of dresses for church, and a few casual outfits. If I had known what was about to happen, I would not have gone home and would have been better prepared to stay.

Even after 20 years, it is still unthinkable that one person could do this to another, no matter how they felt about them. The drive to my parents took two days, and the first day was awkward. He kept silent, and I knew the other woman occupied his mind.

I sought to be lighthearted. I determined that when he discovered an admirable trait in myself, that his affection for her would wane.

The second day was horrific. He was silent for the first few hours, and then he announced his intention to leave me at my parents' and return to his girlfriend. I realized that our situation could improve, but I hoped to resolve our issues and fulfill God's design for our lives.

When I asked him to clarify, he reminded me of his recurring denials of love and his numerous requests that I leave. He indicated that I had the pastor's support and his admonition to stay.

His next words were like a knife wound. He informed me that our relationship was over and that he was leaving me to be with "her." I broke down, sobbing, questioning why he couldn't love me, but he told me to shut up. At that moment, I felt the impact of all the heartache through the years, and I couldn't gain my composure.

He threatened that if I did not stop crying, he would take me to the mountains, shoot me, and leave my body where I couldn't be found. I believe God strengthened me because I managed to calm down.

For the next few hours, I focused on merely surviving, seeking to fulfill his every whim. He compelled me to act seductively, which made me feel like a cheap thrill. I was unaware of it at the time, but I now realize how treacherous it was.

He had threatened me just a few hours before, but I wasn't thinking perceptively. I couldn't accept the reality that 13 years of life and togetherness was gone.

What came next is still a blur, but my parents remember our arrival. He placed my bags on their porch, handed me my dog and the keys to my car. He walked away, with someone evidently waiting nearby to pick him up.

My next memory is of his family inviting me to come for a final Thanksgiving dinner, only to treat me as a mockery and a laughingstock. They didn't end their ridicule after the holiday. I received heartless, demeaning letters, unsympathetic of how crushed I was. Eventually, I had to ask that they let me be.

I don't remember much about the next couple of months, except frequent tears, excruciating migraines, and dreadful sorrow. My friends have recollections and pictures of times we spent together, but the photos seem like someone else's life.

During the Christmas season, I felt isolated. My parents were supportive, but churches were busy with activities, and people were not readily available. One evening in early spring, my spouse called and asked if I wanted to come home. I questioned if he was willing to let his girlfriend go, and he said no, that he only called me because the pastor insisted. I replied that I could not walk back into that situation. He reasoned that if I would only lose some weight and begin to dress carnally, his love for me would grow, and we could resolve our issues.

I told him that my relationship with God was too valuable to go back on my convictions and that I would not submit myself to that type of treatment again.

I made my last goodbyes and began trying to put my life back together. Supposedly he had paid the car off and the insurance six months in advance, but I felt that I should confirm the situation.

The car payment and insurance were, in fact, several months in arrears. I didn't have a job and couldn't figure out how I would make it. I managed to find a decent job with fair pay, and I made arrangements with the car payment. Those two bills were requiring my entire paycheck, but having the car was a necessity.

One evening at church, the evangelist preached that making sacrifices would result in God's blessings. I had $500 in my billfold for the next car payment, and I kept feeling led to give it. The minister repeatedly encouraged everyone to lay their offerings on the platform, but I had no other way to make that payment.

I wasn't sure what to do. I owed $1500 on the car, and I was still three months behind. The evangelist said, "Someone has $500 in your billfold, and you need to bring it to the altar," so I did! Terrified and tearful, I laid it all on the altar.

The next morning I called the loan company to inform them that my $500 payment would be late. They expressed confusion and said that I didn't owe them $500. They stated that instead, they owed me $1500! God performed a miracle!

In another instance, my spouse requested my W-2 forms to file the taxes. Even though I had made unwise decisions in the past, I realized that this was wrong, and I adamantly refused. He became enraged to the extent that I was convinced that he would attempt to kill me.

He verbally assaulted me and reminded me of all the bills I had "left him with." I asked for my pastor's guidance, and he advised that I should not give him any money under any circumstances.

I ultimately decided I had had enough. I fell on my face in my walk-in closet and cried out to God at length. I committed myself to serve God at all costs. A spiritual transformation took place, and I have never been the same.

Of course, I have failed and made mistakes and come short of the glory of God, but God has been faithful. I have found Him to be everything I ever needed. After a few years, my heart started to mend, and my spouse filed for divorce. Signing the papers was difficult, but I did it. I surrendered it all to God. He married the girlfriend within a couple of years, and I haven't heard from him since. I've come in contact with his family, and they blamed me, but that's okay.

A good friend eventually introduced me to someone who had previously been very sick and thus hadn't ever dated. We began talking, and I handled the relationship carefully and prayerfully.

He asked me to marry him after we had dated for a while. He called it courting. I was afraid to accept his proposal because of the mistakes I had made in the past, but my family and friends assured me that he loved me and would not take advantage of me.

We were married on a late summer morning, and I began a new journey with a man who loves me more than he loves life itself. After four years, we adopted a beautiful, two-day-old baby girl, and later a 16-month old little girl. Our last adoption was a four-month-old little boy.

Writing this story was very difficult and conveyed the feeling of walking out of the fire into an oasis. I'm not pretending that circumstances have been perfect or that there haven't been struggles, but our marriage doesn't include abuse, abandonment, or being asked to leave. We are, without a doubt, there for each other.

God has blessed me immensely, and through it all, I have gained compassion for those that are brokenhearted. I bear no grudges. God has eradicated the sense of trauma and has been the center of my joy.

Isaiah 35:1-2 says, "The wilderness and the solitary place shall be glad for them; and the desert shall rejoice, and blossom as the rose. It shall blossom abundantly, and rejoice even with joy and singing: the glory of Lebanon shall be given unto it, the excellency of Carmel and Sharon, they shall see the glory of the Lord, and the excellency of our God."

I met Sis. Kathy Corson many years later, and I felt drawn to her and Bro. Corson. Anytime she was in a revival nearby, I attended. In time she shared her desire to begin a ministry dedicated to abused women, and I helped her pray about it.

The first LAMPS conference was in Longville, Louisiana. It was on a cold, wintry day, January 16, 2016. What a phenomenal service. I shared a portion of my story and was amazed at the healing I received. That morning I stepped off the platform an entirely new person.

I had been to many conferences, trying to move forward, but I was in a rut. I had harbored so much pain and didn't feel I could receive deeper healing.

In that LAMPS service, I was enabled to release the pain and progress in the healing process. It was incredible. Three days later, I continued to bask in God's presence. It was as if I were walking on a cloud.

Now, several years later, LAMPS has been an enormous part of my life, and I have received healing in many different ways. LAMPS is a ministry of deliverance. I have since witnessed a multitude of women receive healing, deliverance, and freedom from bondage.

I owe everything to God for his healing and all he has done for me, but I also desire to honor Sis. Corson for her burden and vision for wounded women.

Writing this has been a healing process also, and I pray that my story helps you. Even if your significant other hasn't hit you doesn't mean you're not in a dangerous situation. If you are in a relationship that seems unsafe, hostile, or dangerous, please seek help and find safety.

Chapter 5 by C.M. Daughter of M.M.

Never Too Young

My journey is a little different from others. In the few months before I started going to LAMPS, I had witnessed the drastic changes in my mother's life. I was skeptical, however, considering it focused on past abuse.

I was a mature 11-year old at the time, and I naturally thought only of physical abuse. Since I hadn't been through that, I assumed I wasn't qualified to go. I learned from my mom that there were other types of abuses that people deal with, such as spiritual, mental, self-abuse, etc.

As a young person looking back into my past, I realized that I had experienced abuse. It wasn't the most typical abuse, but I had struggled with painful situations, even as a young child.

In February of 2018, I decided to attend my first LAMPS service with my mom. I would never have imagined what was in my near future, but I have never been the same.

I'm so thankful. I believed myself to be too young and shy, but God called me out of that. I have grown more abundantly in Him and have found purpose in His kingdom, even as a youth.

I pray that every young person has the opportunity to be a part of a ministry like this when they need it. Youth need help and guidance from their elders.

Of course, I have received much criticism from cynics who claimed that it was silly to believe that I had suffered abuse. One of my favorite questions that I have been asked is, "Are you going to an abuse rehab?" Amusing query, but I then have the opportunity to explain what it actually is, and how it has changed mine and my family's lives.

I choose not to worry about the doubters. If you are willing, God will use you, no matter how old or young you are. Through LAMPS, I have met many exceptional elders and younger people as well from different places.

I know God is still writing my story, but I am thankful for those he has placed in my life through LAMPS and the possibilities to lend service and support.

Chapter 6 by L.W.M.

From the Preacher's Home

While I feel somewhat hesitant to share this story, I feel compelled to press forward simply because I know I am not the only one who has been or will face similar circumstances. It is NOT meant to cast any disparaging shadows over my upbringing but merely to shed light on the power, mercy, and saving grace of our Lord Jesus!

I was always lively and talkative, and I 'never met a stranger.' Therefore, I believe that God had already equipped me with the ability to press through what I would ultimately face in my future.

My parents loved me. There was no doubt about that because I always had all my needs met. We consistently had food on the table, clothes on our backs, and a roof over our head. I grew up in relatively meager circumstances, but I never realized we were poor because my parents didn't discuss it. My parents raised us to have faith in a God who always provided.

However, you can have all your physical needs met, be taken to church regularly, taught to pray and have faith, how to live for God, and yet still be subject to abuse. I deplore that word.

While I did not understand then that it was "abuse," I look back now and realize implicitly the abuse I suffered. It was mostly verbal.

There was some physical abuse, but not what I would consider "stereotypical." I will later delve further into this portion of my story.

We have all heard the adage, "sticks and stones may break my bones, but words will never hurt me," but nothing could be further from the truth. It was instilled in us to be tough and to "let words roll off like water off a duck's back." However, words DO hurt. Words STICK to you.

Words affect your life for a long time! I know this first hand because of things that were spoken to me so regularly that I grew up believing them! To be transparent, being called a "hare-brained idiot" causes you to think that is all you'll ever be. I vowed early in life that if I ever had children, that was one word they would never hear roll off my tongue towards them.

I think I was about 3 or 4 years old when I first remember physical pain exacted upon me. We were at church, and honestly, I have no idea what I had done to deserve it, but I was backhanded across the face causing my nose to bleed. Mom rushed me to the restroom and tried to stop the bleeding.

A few years later, after I was in school, I remember sitting at our kitchen table. I was trying to do some math homework, and Dad was helping me. Because of his anger, I was already tense, so I could not focus on the math problem enough to figure it out. He would yell out that nasty word, "idiot," causing me further distraction and angst. The longer I took to figure out the math problem, the angrier he became until he finally slapped me.

During my grade school years, I was often on the honor roll with excellent grades, but too many times, I got lousy conduct marks for talking too much. I was afraid to bring my report card home because my parents didn't appear to notice my high scores, only the negative conduct marks.

What they viewed as entirely negative ultimately revealed itself to be a blessing in disguise as I grew into my young adult years and beyond. It is not everyone's forte to stand in front of large crowds and speak, but it is truly easy for me. Who would have envisioned that back then?

There were instances when my dad would be working on our vehicle, and I would be his "helper." He was a great shade-tree mechanic, and that saved us money. He would tell me which tools he wanted and send me scurrying to his toolbox on the back porch. I would search diligently and either return with the wrong one or come back saying I could not find it. You have probably guessed it; he would start on his tirade of yelling and calling me a stupid idiot!

It felt like I could never do anything right in his eyes. However, through it all, I DID learn the right tools and could even change oil and spark plugs in my vehicles. Being the oldest of three girls, it seemed like I got in trouble for everything, even if I was not directly involved with their shenanigans. Since there are no manuals on "how to raise children," I was told they had to learn with me. How grand it felt to be the family "guinea pig."

I never felt a warm and tender embrace assuring me I was daddy's girl, or even any affection from my mom. I KNEW they loved me, but it was never physically shown to me. I never heard words of affirmation. I never was told they were proud of me for my accomplishments.

Most of the physical attention I got was getting a whipping almost every time we got home from church because it seemed I was always getting in trouble. I began to be consumed by fear that whatever I did was either not good enough or wrong.

My dad never told me that I looked pretty but would instead find something wrong with my appearance. I could share multiple situations of ill-treatment, to which some of you readers would surely be able to relate. I will share a few more as I continue sharing my story.

Before I move on, I want to interject something vitally important. I was baptized in Jesus' Name in our home church at the age of 9. I did not receive the Holy Ghost until I was 11, and that was while we lived in another state that we had moved to, so my parents could help their friends who pastored there.

We moved a lot due to my dad being a minister/pastor. During these moves to other states, I saw my dad become even more of an angry man, and his anger lashed out so many times, not only to me but to my mother.

I had to watch him continually put her down, calling her many derogatory names. Of course, as a child, I was unaware that he was suffering from terribly low self-esteem. Experiencing his fury, and besides, witnessing him unleash it on my mom, also contributed to tearing down my self-worth.

I cannot tell you how many times my sisters and I would huddle together in the night as we heard him screaming disgusting insults to her and even threatening her that if she tried to leave, he would break her legs. He told her on several occasions to kill herself.

There were times I tried to intervene bodily and received a beating for it. There were times when my sisters and I were so scared of his behavior that we would call 9-1-1 and have a police officer show up at our home.

It is utterly embarrassing calling the authorities on your father, when he is a minister or pastor. Moreover, it is mind-boggling that he could stand behind a sacred desk on Sunday or Wednesday, preaching under an anointing, and then behave in such a vile manner in the home.

Another vivid instance happened at the age of 11. I got into trouble for something that I cannot remember, and my dad lost his temper. He grabbed a belt and began to beat me across my back with the buckle, leaving bloody whelps.

It got so out of hand that my mom had to pull him off me, and he then turned on her. She helped me get a bath, and I recall hearing her break down and cry because of how my back looked. The water on my back felt like fire.

While I endured this type of so-called discipline, my dad was also known as the neighborhood clown. All the neighbors' kids loved him because he would always get out in the yard and play games with them. They never knew the side of him that I had to see almost daily.

It was sad that he acted so fun-loving outside our four walls, even though he was a different creature in the privacy of our home. However, it was clear that we all tried to shield anyone from ever knowing or seeing that side. People viewed us as the "perfect family."

As I began to transition into my teens, I began to have a greater desire for attention. Sadly, because I did not receive proper attention growing up, I began to accept any attention I could get from boys. I never had many boyfriends to speak of, even until I married my first husband. We had moved back to Texas and back to our home church, where I started having a few interests.

Those relationships fizzled quickly, leaving me feeling less than desirable. Then there was my first real boyfriend! He was 18 months younger than me, but that did not matter because he was fulfilling a need, and he made me feel beautiful. He made my heart melt. Due to him not being fully IN the church, I could not associate with him, but I found ways to sneak around and see him anyway. Our parents finally accepted our status and gave us more freedom to be together. That unfortunately led to immoral behavior between us.

Despite knowing better, it was amazing to feel what I thought was "love" and I did not try to stop the behavior.

This relationship lasted for about a year, and then we moved once more for my dad to take a pastorate. There again, we had encounters with police officers at our home due to domestic violence.

It was common by this time to have things broken from being slammed or chunked across the room. My dad would become so enraged that the sounds he made were indescribable, and the veins in his neck looked as if they would burst.

In just a matter of moments, he moved from being enraged to complete calm. How could he transform so quickly? Nevertheless, those "words" made their mark, an indelible mark, that would leave us scarred for life.

I broke up with my boyfriend, but about a year and a half later, after graduation, we reconnected and resumed our relationship.

Much older now, we decided to be together no matter what our parents said. We found ourselves sexually active before marriage.

Yes, I said it! A preacher's daughter, gone bad. When my dad, who was our pastor, discovered that we had fallen into sin, along with another engaged couple who found out that they were expecting a baby, he publicly shamed us all during service from behind the pulpit. It caused such humiliation the other couple left the church. Even after becoming a married young lady, his verbal abuse did not stop.

I could go on and on about the years of the verbal abuse that continued. How did I survive all that and remain living for God? To put it simply, I held on! I had been rooted and grounded in the truth enough for myself that I KNEW I had no other options. I did have a healthy fear of God, and for that, I am forever thankful.

I remained married for 16 years, and God gave me four beautiful children. That marriage ended in divorce even after trying to keep it together. Sadly, it took me falling into an adulterous relationship to blow the cover from my now ex-husband. He had been cheating on me for years.

I will never forget what a dear minister friend of ours told me years after our divorce. He had tried on countless occasions to mentor him and told him, "Son, if you do not treat her like your wife instead of a child, you will eventually lose her."

His response still makes me shudder today. "Ah, she's a preacher's kid; she'll hang." I was honestly so naïve, and he knew very well he could take advantage of that and get by with it.

It became apparent while attending marriage therapy, and after experiencing a nervous breakdown, there would not be a reconciliation. So we filed for divorce. One year after the divorce was final, I DID marry the man that I had fallen with. Now you are probably wondering how I could do that and still hope for God's blessings? Not in the least did I expect God's blessings; however, what I DID experience was His Grace, Mercy, and Forgiveness.

We just celebrated our 20th anniversary. I would claim that we beat the odds, but it did not happen with ease nor without many trips to the altar. There have been some incredibly dark days, and divorce almost happened several times. But God!

I was privileged to attend my first LAMPS conference at our local church in 2017, which is one that I shall forever have composed in the annals of my heart. I had faced many dark times and other current, overwhelming problems, but I had a spiritual experience that I had never had, even though my parents raised me in the church.

I was worshipping in the first service. Both Sis. Kathy Corson and Sis. Jenifer Williams ministered to me, giving me the same concise "word" from God. That was momentous, considering they had not conversed before ministering to me.   That night I remember leaving late. The service went way longer than expected because the spirit was moving so powerfully. When I finally settled in and went to bed, I began to feel sick, so I prayed. I knew I didn't have time for sickness.

I got up a couple of times to try and feel better, but the third time I laid down, I vividly remember a bizarre feeling taking place like chills were swirling like a tornado inside my body.

Within an instant, it felt like someone pulled a plug from my feet, and this swirling sensation drained out until it was all gone. I laid there in a daze, but immediately I KNEW that something had left my body. I couldn't wait to get back and share with the ladies. Not only did I receive a measure of emotional healing but in that next service Sis. Corson came directly to me and spoke into my spirit, although she was unaware of what was taking place at home.

The Spirit of God hit me mightily. I danced gracefully (which has never been my norm) across the entire front of the church. I stopped dancing but continued to worship, and I noticed that the tongue I was speaking in was different than my usual dialect and came from an unusually greater depth of my being.

All these experiences transformed me forever. I attended several more LAMPS conferences after that. Each one continued to bring many more necessary changes and emotional healing into my being! Thank you, Jesus, for LAMPS!

What I want to leave you with is how I am still standing today. There is only ONE answer to that question. I CLUNG to JESUS! Even when my heart was not right, I NEVER missed one church service aside from illness.

I KNEW where my lifeline was. I also knew I had four sets of eyes watching me, and their futures relied on my choices. I could live for God or not, but to walk out on God meant walking out on my heritage and my children, which were to be recipients of that heritage. While I have indeed suffered a genuine identity crisis, trying to find my worth from people, I have finally learned to accept my identity in Christ. I am NOT who or what they said I was. I also learned to forgive!!!

To all the preacher's kids out there who can relate, please understand you CAN survive and make it IF you hold on to Jesus!

Chapter 7 by D.B.

Jesus Loves Me

The first scripture that I ever read was Jeremiah 29:11-13, which states: "For I know the thoughts that I think toward you, saith the LORD, thoughts of peace, and not of evil, to give you an expected end. Then shall ye call upon me, and ye shall go and pray unto me, and I will hearken unto you. And ye shall seek me, and find me, when ye shall search for me with all your heart."

I lived with my mom until I was almost 13. There were always varied types of abuses taking place. My mom raised both my brother and me, but I also had a sister that did not live with us.

My mother was involved with witchcraft, and performing satanic ceremonies, so we moved every two or three months, all over the United States. I have lived in every state except for seven. There was always a group of 13 people that she traveled with, and during these ceremonies, they performed human sacrifices. She explained that we frequently moved because your social security number could track you if you worked a job for too long, and she was always on the run.

My brother and I learned not to make friends with anyone because of our moving so often. We always knew we were going to have to leave. We grew to be each other's best friend.

My mother was always emotionally distant, and she would forget to feed us, so we would usually steal groceries from the store to have something to eat. One of us would be on the lookout while the other stole the items so that we didn't get caught.

We didn't always know what we were stealing, so sometimes it would be something like cream of mushroom soup, and we would eat it straight out of the can.

She would often go into a place like McDonald's to get food for herself, but she would make us eat leftovers from the trash can. My brother and I would sometimes eat dog food off of the neighbor's porch, and my brother would say, "Oh, we can pretend we're eating pizza or ice cream."

We were so hungry all the time. I always wondered what my mom's reasoning was for not feeding us. She cooked well for the men she had around, like steaks, but it was never for us. When the state removed us from our mother, they compared the way we lived to gypsies.

My mother was always with a different man. When I was 13, and saw court records, she had already had seven last names. I'm not sure how many times she was married after that.

My mother allowed some of her husbands to abuse me however they liked. My mother also abused us mentally, physically, and sexually, including making us do sexual things to her and to each other. If she were low on money, she would also prostitute me out to men. I am still not a very affectionate person, although I've grown more so. Because of the sexual abuse, my relationship with my husband has been affected.

One time we were living in an A-frame house in Washington State. Sometimes we would be asleep, and my mother would come into the room in the middle of the night, for no reason, and start beating me.

I would often sleep on my stomach, and she would beat me on my back and claim that God told her to do it. She would make us tell her, "Thank you," and if we didn't, the beating would get worse. My brother would comply, but I was very stubborn and would refuse to say it.

My brother and I shared a room upstairs, and there was paneling on the walls. Because of my mother's frequent rampages and abuse, my brother put a hole in the wall so that we could put a plug through it for a lamp and could store things such as the stolen food.

The attic had two sides, and you could walk around it. We set it up to stay on one side, with a bucket on the other for going to the restroom. Sometimes we would stay in the attic for up to three days and hide, and we had to remain extremely quiet so she couldn't hear us. The abuse was horrendous, and we had no other option.

In my 20's, I began having bad back problems. I ended up going to four different surgeons, and three of them, unaware of my history, said that the issues were from child abuse. I've had to have multiple back surgeries because of it.

When finding this out, it made me feel a fresh hatred towards my mother. It always seemed like she hated us. For some reason, she abused me more than she did my brother, but I was the youngest child. I've heard that sometimes abusers pick specific victims.

She may have suffered from self-hatred, and she may have chosen me because she saw herself in me. I've always wondered what made her the way she was, but she probably had a dreadful childhood, as well. The involvement with witchcraft didn't start with her; it started with her parents and their parents, passing down generational curses.

I never knew my dad. My mother always told me that he was dead, but I found out that he wasn't when I got older. Often I tried to run away from her, so she started cutting the bottoms of my feet with a double-edged razor blade so that I wouldn't run.

When I turned 12, they dedicated me to the devil in a ritual performance. There were seven men around an altar, and they tied me to it and sexually abused me as part of the ceremony.

I didn't get saved until I was 27, and this event haunted me more than any other. We knew that our lives were not typical, and that what was happening was wrong, but our mom always told us that if we confided in anyone, she would kill us. We were afraid to speak out.

My brother and I were taken from my mother when I was 13, and at first, they told us that we were going to get to be together and that they weren't going to separate us.

In our first foster home, an adult male shared marijuana with my brother, and my brother then became addicted to drugs. They removed him and put him into a boy's home, so we became separated.

After that, I became wild, so I ran away from every home they placed me in. I ended up being in eight different foster homes because I was misbehaving and kept running away.

During my teen years, I partied, drank, and did drugs, to forget the memories. I knew that if I could get drunk or high enough that I could forget for at least a little while, but when I woke up the next day, I was facing the same thoughts all over again.

When I was six years old, I got to spend the night with a friend. They took me to church, and I got to go to Sunday School. I didn't dare share that with my mother.

In Sunday School, I remember a little boy singing, "Jesus Loves Me." Scoffing, I asked him why he was singing that, and I informed him that Jesus didn't love either of us.

From that experience, I always remembered that there was a God, and so at the age of 27, being at rock bottom, the memory of that little boy singing "Jesus Loves Me" came back to me.

At this time, I was a single mom with two kids by two different men, and I struggled to make it and take care of my girls. As a foster child, they sometimes forced me to go to church, but I learned to tune it out because I didn't want to be there. It perplexed me that if God loved me, why He had allowed these atrocities to happen to me.

I had gotten to the point that I didn't want to live anymore. I had finally allowed my mom back into my life, and she would apologize over and over and claim that she thought that she had been a good mother, and memories of my past came back to terrorize me. I wanted to end my life, but I decided to look for a church in the phone book.

I found a number for a church and called it. I asked them what I should wear, and they told me to come just as I was. When I arrived for service, someone was singing a special medley of songs, and it "just so happened" that it included "Jesus Loves Me."

It wasn't long after that I got the Holy Ghost. I didn't receive it right away, but it was ultimately the best experience of my life. The church people were very kind to me. They donated clothing because I didn't have any appropriate church clothes.

At the altar call, after you've prayed, it is the norm for people who know some of what you've been through to say, "Now that you've prayed, just leave it on the altar," but it isn't as uncomplicated as that. For years after receiving the Spirit, I was still burdened and obsessed by my past. Seeing or smelling certain things would reawaken my consciousness.

I got into the church, and I also tried going to counseling because I couldn't get freedom from the pervading recollections. Counseling helped somewhat, but not ultimately. I couldn't even go to a Christian counselor because my insurance wouldn't cover them. It took a long time to receive restoration, and I didn't receive it until I went to LAMPS.

I was introduced to the LAMPS ministry by Sis. Vickie Hodges, and every time I went, there would be another layer or aspect of my story that God would uncover. I kept thinking that I had fully overcome, but then there would be something else God would bring to light. It's a process that I've had to work through.

At the first LAMPS, I connected with a few ladies, including Sis. Cathy Talent, and exchanged contact information with her. One day I texted her and thought she might help me with a particular part of my history, specifically when they dedicated me to the devil.

That had continued to torment me immensely, even after receiving the Holy Ghost.

The devil would tell me that the Holy Ghost wasn't real and that I hadn't actually received it. He would remind me of my dedication to him and tell me that God didn't sincerely care for me. Those thoughts endlessly consumed my mind.

After pouring my heart out to Sis. Talent, she would pray with me, and God would embrace me in an overwhelming peace. I will never forget seeing an angel in my room one time during our prayer. Sis. Talent helped me overcome the effects of that traumatic remembrance.

I needed a ministry like LAMPS because of its focus on deep-seated, emotional, and spiritual recovery. It invites you to heal gradually from specific instances as God brings them to the light, one by one. There are probably still circumstances I need to overcome, but I have already received help through the darkest trauma that I have ever faced.

My life was significantly shattered, and I'm so thankful I found the church, but I needed more profound support. At LAMPS, I knew that I wouldn't be alone. I wholeheartedly believe that it has afforded me a quality of spiritual health that I could not have achieved in this amount of time if it wasn't for this ministry.

You can't share much of what you've been through at church because people cannot understand, and you don't want to experience judgment. If I confided in anyone, I feared they would no longer allow their children to play with my daughters.

I'm not sure if that would have been the case, but I kept many things secret for that reason.

At the first church I attended, I didn't closely associate with anyone; I kept everyone only as acquaintances. That was partially because we moved so much as a child, and I didn't welcome intimate relationships. LAMPS has enabled me to make friendships and create deeper bonds with people. I formerly attempted to protect myself by erecting walls.

There was a foot-washing ceremony at one of the last LAMPS services I attended, but I was very opposed to anyone touching my feet. I believed them to be ugly and felt ashamed of them because of what my mom had done to them. Instead of finding a partner to participate in the foot-washing, I helped Sis. Corson so that I could keep my feet from exposure and personal contact.

Towards the end, Sis. Whitney Davis came and found me and said that she wanted to wash my feet. I emphatically told her no, but I finally consented and gave her permission to wash them. Several ladies came around and prayed, and I received a deeper healing that night.

I appreciate Sis. Corson and Sis. Talent for helping me prevail over these issues. The Spirit had already transformed my life, but I remained imprisoned in my mind. Thankfully, however, because of the LAMPS ministry, I have been set free from the strongholds that had control of me.

Chapter 8 by S.R.

He Made Sure I Didn't Forget

I remember my introduction to God at a very early age, with a Bro. Smith teaching us a Bible study at the dinner table. I remember the flip chart he used and how he tried to play his video on our VCR, but he couldn't get it to work. He prayed a simple prayer that the Lord would FIX the VCR! My parents laughed a little, and one of them said that they didn't think God made those kinds of repairs.

If I remember correctly, in the same breath, my parents and Bro. Smith said simultaneously, "Well, He IS GOD!" At that moment, I realized that God could do whatever He wanted to do.

My first memory of someone praying a sincere prayer was when I stepped on a nail while my Daddy and Bro. Smith worked in the yard. I was wearing little, black, lace-up booties. I was lying on my back, and Daddy was trying to get my shoe off. My foot was gushing blood. Bro. Smith laid his hand on me and cried out to God on my behalf. His voice was so loud and deep.

I wasn't sure how to interpret that at the time, but I've never forgotten it. Dad worked with Bro. Smith in the oil field and his pastor's church was not far from my house. He witnessed to Daddy often, and we started attending church at Smoky Cove UPC when I was a young child. My brothers and I were dedicated and attended Sunday School there for several years until my parents divorced.

After my parents' divorce when I was 12, conditions changed dramatically. I was devastated. When we were with my mom, we attended a denominational church, and when we were with my dad, we continued going to a pentecostal church.

To reveal that there was considerable confusion in my mind and heart at that time is an understatement. Regardless, I knew without a doubt that I loved Jesus and that I wanted to go to Heaven!

I have always loved Jesus! For a long season, I spent every moment possible at my mom's church because I was so hungry for God. That was the only place where I didn't feel overlooked. I know my parents loved me, but I didn't feel that way as a teen. I attended so many events that someone in authority once told me that I couldn't spend every second at church!

I was hurt because I didn't want to lose that safe place, and I was puzzled! Shouldn't we always have that level of desire and commitment? When I was 14 or 15, my grandmother was diagnosed with cancer. During that time, she and I both received the Holy Ghost. I can still remember her praying with me at the altar!

I was so delighted to have Jesus. I recall telling the pastor once that I hated leaving church. He replied that, thankfully, we always got to come back. He was right! The church and my grandparents' house were indeed the only places I found peace.

I felt lonely and out of place at home. To further complicate things, I was ill-informed that many of the things I believed in weren't necessary to get to Heaven. My mind became consumed with turmoil because of the religious differences. At school, I found out that a friend had said something very hurtful about me.

A boy in my class confronted me. He mocked and bullied me until I wept on my desk. I struggled with coping, primarily because I didn't know how to touch God through His Spirit at that time.

Not long after, my grandmother passed, and then I mostly gave up. I gave up on church, not on God, but I decided that I would fall short anyway, so I might as well quit. I lacked clarity of what was right. Being bullied was crushing, and I already felt like my circumstances were more than I could handle.

At 16, I started dating my first boyfriend and engaged in a sinful relationship that lasted for a couple of years. After that relationship ended, I faced several life-changing situations. As previously mentioned, I was already struggling with sexual immorality. I then encountered a guy I knew from school. He hadn't liked me then, but suddenly, I found myself the subject of his interest.

His attention was flattering, and we soon began a very unhealthy relationship. During our time together, I was negatively influenced and even FORCED to do unimaginable things. I was verbally, emotionally, and physically abused. At one point, I remember telling God how sorry I was to be in the place to witness such things.

Once I mentally resolved to escape the chaotic situation I was in, God once again intervened for me. We usually had to lift our front trailer door to level it to close and latch it. I can't remember why, but my cousin, who had cancer, had gone there with me. He and my boyfriend were arguing, and he started to hit my cousin. I got in the way, and he came after me. He had a crazy look in his eyes, and I knew he would hurt me if I didn't get away.

By providence, I ran into the house and flung the door closed! It shut and latched (without having to adjust it as was usual). I locked it properly, got out through the back, and jumped in the vehicle without him seeing me.

I was in amazement. I had an intense perception that God was with me in my situation that night, but after that, my self-confidence began to plummet. Over the next couple of years, I had so little self-worth that I rebounded from one boyfriend to another while being introduced to drug after drug.

I felt so hollow. I already used tobacco and alcohol, and then it quickly became pills, cocaine, and methamphetamine. The bizarre thing is, I didn't pursue any of these things! I never paid for any of it, and by the grace of God, I never had to trade myself to get it.

I remember lying down at night so often, and I would beg God not to allow me to die lost. I met my oldest daughter's dad at the age of 20, addicted to meth, and I discovered I was pregnant just before I turned 21.

When I saw the positive pregnancy test, I slid down the wall and cried out to God. I had just used meth, but I pleaded with God. I said, "God, if you will please allow my baby to be fine, I won't touch it again," and I didn't during my pregnancy.

While I was pregnant, my daughter's dad went to jail for a short time. After that, we decided to start attending church at DeRidder UPC. It was there that we met an older couple that began giving us Bible studies.

At age 21, I gave birth to a beautiful and healthy baby girl. She was perfect, and I stayed clean for a while. We soon separated, however, and I once again began to use drugs and drink excessively.

Over the next couple of years, I put myself and my daughter in positions that later shamed me. One night we were at my grandpa's house, and we got into bed and got ready for sleep. While looking at my perfect, sleeping daughter, I prayed a prayer that completely broke my heart. I implored God to protect my little girl from anything that would hurt her, even if it was me. God honored that prayer, and he soon began to reconstruct my life.

He must have thought she needed me because he saved both of us from drowning when she was less than two years old.

One pitch-black and rainy evening, a guy I was involved with accidentally drove my car into the Sabine River, with us inside. "Coincidentally," there were people there that could help. It was indeed a miracle.

After that accident, God began to remove people and things from my life. Not quite a year later, I married my first husband. While the relationship was not ideal, God began to refine my life. I was still using tobacco and drinking heavily, but for the most part, I quit using drugs!

During that time, I met one of my very best friends and sisters in the Lord. I loved her almost immediately, and I know that she began praying for me! She also began to witness to me! My husband and I desperately struggled financially, and we fought a lot! As his drinking worsened, God started to deal with me profoundly. We started attending Longville UPC in 2010, and on December 5, 2010, I received the Holy Ghost baptism! It was glorious!

I remember it felt like hot water cascading over my head. I had the impression that if I stepped to the side, that I would step out of the puddle of sin that had just melted away! From that point forward, I pursued God with every breath! The more I sought after Him, the worse my marriage became. The more I prayed for my husband's salvation, the more vigorously he fought it.

The clash for my soul was not over. My husband disliked my regular church involvement because he didn't like going. He and others told me often that I needed to spend more time at home with him, but I no longer wanted to live that way.

I didn't want to drink and party anymore; I despised how I felt when I lived that kind of life. I hungered after Jesus! The greater Jesus used me, the more desperate my circumstances became. I ultimately began to pray that God would move my husband out of the way if he weren't going to submit to God.

I honestly did not expect that to happen. I sincerely believed that my husband would repent and submit. I was so distraught because I longed for him to change, but it was not to be.

God began to bring certain scriptures to my attention, giving me direction and fashioning a plan in His divine way! Two weeks later, my husband decided to leave me, but God had prepared me. I accepted it and chose to trust in God.

Meanwhile, I didn't have a job. I had a vehicle, but it didn't have a heater. I had no place to live, but I needed to provide for my ten-year-old daughter! We had endured great difficulties, but once again, God intervened! Within a few days, someone gave me a camper. Within weeks, I had a job, and within a few months, a brand new car.

Even with all of God's provisions, I still suffered from hurt and loneliness. The enemy then sent a diversion to steal my vision! I should have learned by then, but I developed a new relationship that God did not intend.

Fortunately, I hadn't backslidden yet, and I was wise enough to pray about my situation. I prayed that God would not allow me to enter into another marriage that He did not ordain. I prayed specifically for a husband that would be precisely what I needed. I prayed for everything imaginable concerning what I desired in a husband, including looks, personality, attitude, etc.

When I wrote the details of that prayer, I was in the process of backsliding. It was a slow fade! During this time, I kept telling my church family and my daughter (who was still attending church) and diligently praying for me that this was not the end!

I assured everyone that I desired to live for God but that I didn't feel ready. I encouraged them that I loved God and that I would return to Him!

The following year I met my husband, the one who was the answer to my petition! It seemed as if I was on God's mind when God created him! God renewed me in the Holy Ghost within the year. One morning, early, the pastor and some of the sisters met me at the church. God met me, as well, and I received a renewal in the Spirit!

I was pregnant at this time. The battle raged on. It was challenging to find time to pray and read the Word while having a baby and a toddler, and going to church also took a lot of effort. Hauling all of the baby items and the attention babies demand took most of my focus. My walk with God must be more deliberate now than it used to be.

I have realized that I cannot be the wife and mother I need to be if God isn't at the center. My life cannot be joyful without Jesus, and nothing else is worth teaching my children about other than Him! I recognize that they will not be able to get through this life without Him! I refuse to stand before God and have to admit that I did not teach them about Him.

It has been my experience that my days go more smoothly and peacefully when I keep Jesus first, even when I am weary. I have learned that making prayer a priority every day is crucial and that I must find ways to delve into God's Word. God has blessed me with people that encourage me, and I am dependent upon it.

I have had incredible teachers, such as Pastor and Sis. Talent, and Sis. Kathy Corson of the LAMPS ministry. They consistently share words of wisdom and never fail to be truthful with me, even when it's hard to hear. It is vital to have such people in our lives, to help us determine the right course.

We will always be in a war for our souls. I still make mistakes and need to grow spiritually, but I am resolved to strive for the prize!

Admittedly, throughout my life, there has always been an ongoing struggle for my soul. Nonetheless, I was introduced to God as a child, and He made sure that I would never forget that connection and that I would always recognize His actions on my behalf. He made sure I would always remember where to run!

I found it remarkable to date someone, only to find out his parents had the Holy Ghost! Another example is that I would be somewhere drinking or getting high, and I would discover in conversations with others that they had either been raised in the church or may have even have had the Holy Ghost.

Somehow, in many of these conversations, we would end up discussing God. Looking back, it is clear that Jesus pursued after me, even into places of depravity, and I am so grateful. Except for God's grace, I don't know where I would be.

Life usually has a way of knocking you down and bringing discouragement. If we allow spirits to have free reign, confusion will take control of our children's minds. If we don't lead them on the right path, the world's influence will dominate.

I know by my own experience that how we speak to them and about them is critical! They will take our words to heart. I speak from personal experience that peer pressure at all ages is a tenacious, damaging influence that can have long-lasting effects.

I understand what it's like to be a young adult that longs desperately for Jesus but has no authentic spiritual direction. I am a shining example of the importance of praying for our young people and adults! I relate to addiction taking control of my life and how frenzied you become to feed that addiction. I know how pathetic and dirty you feel and how hopeless things seem!

Thankfully, because of my addiction, I did learn not to judge people too harshly. Having unhealthy relationships, I realized that you never really know what you would do until you're faced with the same decision. I try to avoid saying, "If that were me..."

The actuality is that it takes God to help you break free from addictions and toxic relationships and to help you discover your value!

As a young mother with addictions, I'm so thankful that God got my attention and placed a hedge of protection around me. I still face struggles, and there are more days than not that I have to be deliberate in living for God.

I often do what I must do because I know it's what I should do, not because I feel like it! Even now, I have to face hard decisions, and the devil works hard to distract me. Despite that, however, because of my past, I recognize it for what it is.

My prayer is that God continually empowers us with clear spiritual discernment and perception. We will always have a spiritual battle to fight! Satan will always be at work to destroy us, but Jesus will never let go of us if we are determined never to let go of Him!

People may disappoint us at times, but God never will! I pray that we will earnestly desire to flourish spiritually. Let us give ourselves more fervently to His kingdom than we ever have to the world!

Chapter 9 by L.L.

I Forgave & I'm Forgiven

I'm sharing my testimony of how God helped me through a devastating circumstance as a small child and how it hindered my life.

I desire to remain anonymous because I have forgiven the man for what he has done. He has grandchildren and great-grandchildren living for God, and I do not wish to cause them distress.

I was seven years old at the time of my abuse. The man in question didn't go to church, but his sweet wife did, and my grandmother lived across the street from them. We felt comfortable walking freely all over town, and one day my mom sent me on an errand.

When I got near his house, he beckoned for me to come and help his wife. I stepped inside the house, and he told me she was in another room. When I entered the room, he walked in behind me and shut the door. Confused, I stated that his wife wasn't in there.

He walked up to me and put his hand over my mouth and nose, told me to be quiet and not to yell. I became utterly overwhelmed with fear. He laid me on a table and began to undress and abuse me. I was screaming in great dread, but no sounds were coming out of my mouth.

Just after this began to happen, there was a knock on the front door. He told me to be still. No child or anyone should ever have to confront that kind of FEAR!

I heard a voice penetrate my horror, and it said, "Get up and run NOW!" I heard it repeated twice more, and I got up. I could hear the man talking to someone at his front door. I looked down the hall to the kitchen, and I saw that the back door was open. All that was between myself and freedom was a screen door.

As I ran to the door and opened it, he told me to stop, but that propelled me outside, heart pounding. I remember running, but my feet didn't seem to be touching the ground.

It felt as if someone carried me. I rushed around the house and saw my granny sitting on her doorstep; I raced to her, panic-driven. She asked me if I was hurt. I explained that I wasn't hurt, but I disclosed what had happened. She acknowledged that she understood what I was talking about but said, "We don't talk about such things."

I was devastated that she wouldn't listen to me. I then surmised that if she wouldn't discuss it, that my mother probably wouldn't either. That transformed something inside of me. At the tender age of seven, I learned that men were untrustworthy. I became suspicious of them, and my thinking patterns changed.

I became very protective of my baby sister. We would see the man who had abused me walking down the road, and I walked on the opposite side of my mom. Once he tried to give my sister a dime; I told him sharply that she didn't need his money. My mom scolded me, but I reiterated that she didn't need it. I refused to apologize to him.

Years later, God informed me that it was He who had spoken to me, sent that knock on the door, and prompted me to get out of the house. He also revealed other things to me about Himself during that time.

Sometime after the incident, my friend stood behind the school cafeteria's open door one day, staring through the crack. I asked her if she was okay, and she said, "He's out there." I looked through the gap and saw HIM, walking up and down the school sidewalk.

I said, "He tried to hurt you, too?" She turned and looked at me, and I explained that he had tried to hurt me as well. I put my arm around her in comfort; we didn't speak of what he had done, but I let her know that I was there for her.

One day not long after, I encountered another man sneaking around my cousin's empty house. I recognized him, but I was wary, and I became vigilant. He tried to persuade me to follow him into the vacant house, and I noticed the other man who had abused me was lurking around as well. I got the impression that they were together. Thankfully I managed to keep my distance and escape.

I felt strongly that these two men were working as a team to prey upon young girls. I shared the situation and my feelings about it with my friend and warned her to stay away.

What eight-year-old little girl has that kind of perception? Unfortunately, one who had learned by experience to be suspicious and distrustful of all men, but also a protective one.

Again, years later, God revealed that my keen discernment of the victimization came from Him.

One day my mom and a neighbor were talking about my abuser. He shot himself because he was dying of cancer. He survived but suffered a while before passing away. I hadn't quite turned nine at this time, but I remember looking at my mom and telling her that I was glad that he was dead.

My mom scolded me and told me that speaking like that wasn't acceptable. I eventually confided in her what had happened, and she was puzzled why I hadn't initially confessed. I explained to her that I had told my granny, who wouldn't listen, and that I figured she wouldn't listen, either. She assured me that she would have.

Over the years, I had little trust in boys or men. I determined that none of them would ever be allowed to cause that kind of terror within me again. I became a fighter and refused to take abuse. It has taken me years to realize that some men are trustworthy.

I have a gift for discernment that I wasn't aware I had while growing up, which helped guide me in making sound judgments. God progressively taught and revealed wisdom unto me even as a child, teenager, and still today as an adult.

I backslid for several years, and I was a single parent with children, but I have now been back in church for over 12 years. Three years after praying through, God began to deal with me about the different forms of the word "FORGIVE." I studied the definitions of FORGIVING, FORGIVEN, FORGIVE, and FORGAVE, and their biblical usage.

One day I felt an unction to go to the church and then to the altar to pray about what He was showing me. As I was praying, God spoke to me and said, "If you want to enter Heaven, you have to forgive."

I knew that He was talking about the person who had hurt my friend and me. I told God that I was unsure if I could forgive him, but He repeated that I could only enter Heaven if I were willing to forgive. I prayed for several hours at the altar, sobbing and crying out to God.

I said, "Lord, I want to make it to Heaven. I forgive him." At that moment, I felt a peaceful release come over me, and He revealed to me that it was my granny who had knocked on the door that day. I wept and asked God to forgive me for the bitter feelings that I had harbored against her. I wept for a long time, and I received an unconditional release and healing.

It has now been ten years later. God has taught me to be a giving person in various ways and forgive and not harbor negative feelings against others who have injured me. I thank God for what He has taught me about forgiveness in all of its forms.

I may have stumbled at times, but I haven't stayed down. I get back up and fight (and ask for forgiveness). Jesus has forgiven me of my sins. Satan tries to use the past to overwhelm me, but all victories belong to God.

I am much closer to God than ever before, and I can pray for others that have been through similar situations to be healed and to overcome. I AM AN OVERCOMER with the Lord's help through spiritual guidance, revelation, and direction.

The Lord has shown me how to be a warrior for His kingdom by praying, fasting, and wearing the full armor of God. My faith and trust have grown much more in God, as well as my desire to know Him more fully.

Thank you, God, for forgiving me, and teaching me how to forgive.

Chapter 10 by A.M.

It Saved My Life

I do not remember the message that was preached the night that I was introduced to Sis. Kathy Corson's anointed ministry. However, I am thankful and know that without it, I would most likely be lost today.

At eight years of age, I was sexually abused by my older brother, and then again at 11 by my step-father. During my second marriage, I was verbally abused and also raped.

I do not understand why he raped me. We were married for 50 years, and we were getting along reasonably well. When this happened, it felt like something died inside of me. I was emotionally beat down and lived in a state of depression and oppression.

Then, thankfully, my dear friend invited me to an Inner Circle ladies' meeting. I immediately saw an image of a woman, and I discerned that God was telling me to go.

When I got to the meeting, I saw Sis. Kathy Corson, the woman I had seen in my vision.

I wondered about my purpose for being there, but I knew because of the vision that I had to go.

I realized that purpose, after she ministered to me that night. Through her, I received sufficient hope and strength to share what had happened and let it go.

Chapter 11 by W.D.

Brokenness to Wholeness

Everyone has a story. I am so grateful that the Lord has allowed me this dynamic opportunity to share mine. If it were not for the LAMPS ministry, I honestly do not know where I would be today.

I was a very tortured soul for many years. I can't fathom if, after coming back to God, I could have endured the spiritual abuse I suffered if LAMPS hadn't been founded at the opportune time.

I was on the verge of completely giving up on life, people, and God. LAMPS has enabled me to heal from the inside out, not from the outside in. It has been stated that LAMPS is an acronym that stands for Lives Abused Mentally, Physically, Sexually, Substance, Self, and Spiritually. I am willing to confess that I have experienced them all.

I spent several years of my childhood confused and unstable. When I was in second grade, my male teacher inappropriately handled me several times. I also experienced harassment by one of my mother's boyfriends.

I grew up as a daddy's girl. When I was nine, my dad married his second wife, and he took on the role of being a father to his infant step-daughter. Therefore, living in different zip codes because my mom remarried twice more, I lived away from my dad for the rest of my childhood.

It stands to reason that I lost my trust and hope in man. I was very rebellious in middle school and high school, trying to find something to fill that void. Thank God for a praying family, and that at the age of seven, I received the Holy Ghost and was baptized in the Name of Jesus. By God's merciful hand and amazing grace, He spared me from several suicidal attempts.

LAMPS gave me hope that I was not in my struggles and temptations alone and that others could relate. It is indeed encouraging that you are not the only one that has been through the fire and been burned.

From the age of 16, I entertained the party lifestyle. I became an alcoholic for four years, and that led to other substances as well.

When I was 19, I was in a toxic relationship, and my boyfriend introduced me to DABS. It is one of the darkest and most dangerous drugs available, and I severely hallucinated one night in the car with a group of friends.

After we smoked it, I couldn't feel any bone in my body. I was unable to drive, yet somehow, I made it the 45-minutes home.

Finally, when I couldn't sink any lower or stray any further away from God, I decided it was time to make a change. About seven years ago, at the age of 19, I made the best decision of my life, and I've never turned back.

I am convinced it is because God heard my family interceding for me, along with the call I felt on my life. Everything looked impossible. Every relationship I had was turbulent because I was consumed by guilt and shame. Without any doubt, my worst day living for God is so much better than my best day in the world.

Within a year of being in church, I started facing spiritual abuse. I dealt with unjust persecution-jealousy, being talked about and lied on, in a more significant measure than I ever had in the world. Yet one of my favorite scriptures now is 2 Timothy 3:12, "Yea, and all that will live Godly in Christ Jesus shall suffer persecution."

Suffering persecution is a promise just like the favorable promises that we all desire, such as blessings "pressed down, shaken together, and running over." Becoming involved in the early stages of LAMPS preserved me.

The power from the praying and fasting in advance of each service was phenomenal, pressed down, shaken together, and running over in the Spirit! I learned these steps through this healing process: REVEAL, DEAL, and then HEAL.

When I prayed back through, I was so excited to become involved in a specific ministry I felt very passionate about. I excitedly renewed my skills with a childhood mentor, but sadly, my desire to pursue this ministry was squelched. I was told that this unique calling was not a gift from God, and that being used wasn't necessary, so I just let it go.

Months later, God opened a door, and I had the opportunity to minister in the way I desired at the very first LAMPS Conference! What an honor that was! WOW, the presence of God was more profound than I had ever experienced as a child.

Sis. Corson has treated me like a second daughter in the last six years. She has demonstrated God's love and shared an abundance of wisdom with me. Without her mentorship and the LAMPS ministry, I would not have the relationship with God I have today.

I have ministered at multiple conferences since, including LAMPS, and it has taken me down a journey of healing that I could only ever dream of living.

LAMPS allowed me to experience what it means to love and see people the way God sees them, no matter who they are. Within the last couple of years, my dream has become a reality.

I was a single mother for five years, but I waited on the man that God had for my son and me. We had a gorgeous wedding. The power of God fell, and we spoke in tongues the entire time.

People have expressed that it was fairy-tale-like but probably didn't realize how accurate their statement was. It sincerely was a fairy tale and still is every day.

You do not have to wallow in your guilt and shame daily. You do not have to allow bitterness to destroy your relationship with God and others. You can live in freedom every day!

You are meant to overcome by the blood of the Lamb and the word of your testimony! There is power in forgiveness and allowing God to bring you through. He will bring you out!

It reminds me of the old song that says, "I've been through the fire, but I got out!" My husband and I have faithfully attended a wonderful church together for the past two years, outstanding in its leadership.

You may have to endure a burdensome season such as Joseph did, but there is a specified time and season for everything. God always has a perfect plan because straight is the gate, and narrow is the way. This is the path that leads unto life, but only a few will find it.

I encourage you never to put a time limitation on God. Allow Him to carry you through deep waters so that you become more powerful in God than ever before.

Jesus leaving or forsaking you is not a possibility. He is the author and the finisher of your faith. He knows every facet of your life from birth to death. Despite your mistakes, He is always there with arms wide open, waiting for you to come home.

God's love is unconditional and everlasting. I speak healing tears to flow over you, the reader, right now. Allow God to help you confront truth.

God is faithful in uncovering the issues you have buried inside and empowering you towards a healing journey and a fresh start. In Jesus' Name, Amen.

Chapter 12 by A.N.M.

Recovering Identity

I know beyond all shadow of a doubt that my introduction to the LAMPS ministry was supernatural. I had already received a measure of healing through being vulnerable in God's presence, and allowing His Spirit to flow through me.

However, I still felt an acute rawness inside from lifelong wounds, more rejection than acceptance, and the aftermath of dire familial and other situations. There was an emptiness that grew more profound with each rejection or revelation of the past.

As of this writing, I am in my early 40's, but for the first 34 years of my life, it seemed that my identity was being formed and defined by almost nothing but abuse, hurt, depravity, neglect, rage, and shame.

I certainly realize that wholeheartedly pursuing God has caused me to walk down a completely different path, leading towards healing and wholeness despite my circumstances. Still, without God, I would be hopelessly broken, with no purpose to my pain.

My circumstances caused unfathomable emotional damage from a young age, and I found it very difficult to receive love from God, and from the very few that would seek to reach out to me as an adult.

It's not that I rejected expressions of love, but it didn't seem to penetrate the deadness that I felt. It even appeared that I lost the close connection that I felt to God as a small child, because of the many walls that I continued to build to try and protect myself. So no matter how urgently I cried out to God, (even being filled with God's Spirit), the gaping vacuum in my spirit became even more abysmal.

Feelings of love and joy were foreign to me, to the point that I felt embarrassment and shame as I sought to feel positive emotions. At times different people discerned this, and expressed that it was okay to desire joy, and that I deserved to have joy as much as anyone.

I was unaware that I was internalizing myriad layers of hurt, shame, and, ultimately, bitterness. Even before my earliest memories, I had experienced enough degradation, neglect, and horror to last anyone a lifetime.

It didn't matter that I couldn't comprehend my surroundings; they left their mark anyway. I have described it to others as if, from birth, my experiences were nothing but heaps of rotten garbage piling on top of me. Family dysfunction and generational curses would continue to haunt and impact my life for many years.

I could not find peace, joy or happiness in any area of my life. Even school was a mostly negative experience for me, socially speaking. I experienced a lot of bullying, and while I did have friends at times through the years, it never lasted. I spent many days on the playgrounds or in the cafeteria alone.

My sisters were all quite a bit older than me, and they all (understandably) escaped the nest as quickly as possible, whether they were ready to fly or not. So that left me to face the terrors of our household alone.

My father was not a father by any stretch of the imagination. He was an absolute monster, continually boiling over with maddening and uncontrolled rage. He did provide some of the necessities but made us feel guilty and often revealed tremendous resentment that he had to provide.

I could not wait to escape, and unfortunately, at the tender age of 14, I met a 21-year-old man who would keep me on the roller coaster ride of terror. I did not think of him as a way of escape; I simply thought I had met someone who would love me.

By all appearances, he was the "perfect" guy. He was extremely talented, faithful to church, and very involved in ministry. He was also charming, out-going, adored his mom, and was very knowledgeable of the Word.

He had a calling to preach on his life and was in his last year of Bible college. Our singing voices complemented each other well, and he often told me that he anticipated singing, praying, and ministering together after we got married.

How naive I was, and how severely I lacked the protection of family or spiritual guidance. Yes, there were qualities about him that were true. He was talented. He was faithful to church and involved. I even believe that he was called to the ministry.

Unfortunately, I didn't recognize his proud and arrogant spirit, that the charm was just a facade, or that he was hiding deeply-rooted pain, perverse addictions, and extreme narcissistic behavior.

It took me years to fully realize that he cared much more about being "properly" attired for church than he did about genuine obedience or an authentic relationship with God.

I now understand that my family was under generational curses that had to be broken. It was quite shocking, at barely 17, to believe my life's course was changing for the better and that I had a bright future ahead of me, to almost immediately discover I had made a horrific mistake.

I had married a monster who would reject, terrorize, and abuse me for nearly 20 years. Unfortunately, my children would also suffer from his unloving and cruel treatment, perversity, and lack of being a true father.

My memories as a child, youth, and adult are all significantly void of love, coziness, or anything remotely comforting. Instead, my days consisted of severe emotional insecurities, terror, emotional and physical neglect, rage, and multiple types of abuse.

Any memories of my dad or ex-husband are overwhelmingly of constant, traumatizing turmoil. As I stated earlier, household terrors from birth caused what I can only describe as detrimental emotional detachment and paralysis. I have since learned from older siblings about the environment and circumstances I was born into.

My father was a ruthless man, controlled by dark lusts, addictions and passions, paranoia, constant uncontrollable rage and anger, and a viciously narcissistic personality.

Deep down, I believe he had a love for God and a call to ministry, but he wouldn't forgive, and bitterness ruled every fiber of his being. He allowed Satan and his twisted desires to have free reign in his life.

I know that he suffered undivulged situations as a child, and there were offenses within the church that he couldn't get past. He didn't even try to overcome them, however. He refused to submit to any spiritual authority or seek to be consistent in his spiritual walk.

My father deceived himself that he had uncommon insight into God's Word, despite his inconsistency in living for God. He didn't recognize that while true revelation can be built upon and be more thoroughly understood, it doesn't change fundamentally. He often convinced himself that he had received special revelation, only for that revelation to be completely different a few months down the road.

Because my father refused to forgive and submit, he was always "in and out" of church. Even when he was "in," however, his actions didn't change much. He automatically wanted to be "used" to preach, but wouldn't allow himself to grow or gain deliverance. This added more fuel to his raging anger against the church, believing that everyone was in the wrong except him.

There was one area of his behavior that did change when he was going to church. Instead of teaching right from wrong lovingly or effectively, he would hatefully condemn everyone to hell for behaviors that he had only recently encouraged. He would load up all my older sisters to purchase worldly clothing and other accessories, only to demand that it all be burned a few months later. This pattern played out over and over again.

I will never forget when one of my older sisters borrowed a rock tape from a guy on the bus. My dad found it one day while we were in school. He had never truly taught us anything; he just specified items as worldly and hatefully spewed that we were going to hell.

My sister received a cruel beating with a rope that day, all over her body.

He claimed to love the Word of God, but it seems that he just loved the parts that benefited him (like divine healing). He loved to tout certain doctrines in a spirit of self-pride, and bragged continually about his supposed revealed insight into matters such as prophecy and the doctrine of the Godhead. Unfortunately, he didn't concern himself with practical matters, such as how to treat your family, or getting your flesh under control.

The life he lived caused great havoc in a multi-talented family that could have done great things for God. Instead, because he didn't live or convey the truths of God's Word in a fashion that fosters a love for or relationship with God, he imparted gross bitterness, and left his family with shattered beginnings and tainted perspectives.

When my parents got married, my dad was 27, and my mom was 18. My mom was his sixth wife. He had kids with at least three of the women but was not involved in their lives.

My mom was the first woman that didn't leave him within a few months or years, and so my sisters and I were doomed to be shaped and damaged and scarred by his constant tyranny.

My dad always had a motto that if he wasn't "near the woman he loved," then he just "loved the woman he was near," and he was never ashamed to share that sentiment, even in his older years.

When my parents got married, my dad traveled and worked all over the state. One of his exes told me that I probably have siblings all over the state from his exploits.

I was the fourth and last child of my parents. During my mom's pregnancy with me, my parents received a visit from one of my dad's ex-wives, with a young preteen daughter that my dad didn't know he had. Her mom had been pregnant with her when she left my dad, and she didn't inform him of the pregnancy.

Of course I will never know all of the sordid details, but my father began treating his own daughter as his mistress, violently abusing and raping her. This continued for a couple of years. She later said that she allowed it because she felt it kept him from preying upon the rest of us.

My dad did not try very hard to keep these actions a secret. My oldest full sister, who is only a few months younger than my half-sister, remembers my dad taking her into a bedroom on multiple occasions, where everything could clearly be heard.

My dad was a severe alcoholic at this time, which incited his demons to further depravity. He lived in anger towards everyone, but especially towards my mother, and at the time, he hated her even more for refusing to go to bars and dance and get drunk.

He used that as more of an excuse to be a womanizer and oppressive dictator. He would come home in the middle of the night, screaming, and terrorizing everyone. My oldest full sister remembers seeing him tear off my mother's clothes and violently raping her.

I have been told that I pretty much lived in a crib or playpen in a corner of a back room for the first three years of my life, with little to no interaction. My mom says she was trying to protect me from my father.

My dad loved to go clubbing and drink, and then come home drunk to terrorize his family. He would sit in his truck late at night and loudly rev his engine, terrifying everyone while we were trying to sleep. It thrilled him to foster this constant sense of terror and make us fearfully anticipate his every cruel action.

I do not know if I refused to eat properly, or if it stemmed from the extra turmoil going on at this time, but I lived off of the bottle until I was three, including being put to bed with one, and my teeth were not taken care of. My teeth decayed until I cried night and day with the pain.

My mom fought for me to have my teeth pulled, because they were too far gone to fix. My dad was irate about the paltry sum that he had to pay, but was not concerned about the torment I was in. We had more than sufficient means, but he only liked spending it on himself.

It was nothing for him to buy new vehicles or guns, but we often lived like beggars. Often he informed us how much he hated the fact that we had needs.

Even when my dad didn't go to church, my mother still took us faithfully. I remember being drawn in from a very early age to the worship, singing, and presence of the Lord.

I could be found at the altar at the age of three, crying my heart out. Even though I wasn't acknowledged much by people, I learned that the House of God was a haven. Unable to find comfort, I began to find it in the presence of God, and I learned at an early age to begin seeking Him.

I knew I loved God, deeply. I began to develop a burning hunger to be a worshiper, and to be used by God in every way He desired.

I started singing in church at the age of three. Though it wasn't the norm for a small child of that age to start singing in church during regular services, I believe God created an outlet for me to find some measure of joy and feeling of worth.

From age three until eight, I sought to receive the Holy Ghost, to no avail. No one ever prayed with me or for me or tried to encourage me. Even at church, (except for the presence of God), I felt alone.

One Sunday service, I was worshipping in my pew with all my heart. I wasn't even thinking of receiving the Holy Ghost; I just had my mind on passionately praising God.

All of a sudden, the Holy Ghost came upon me and filled me, and the next thing I knew, I was coming out of a trance-like state, and I knew that I had finally received the Holy Ghost.

I had always sought to be sensitive to the Spirit, although I didn't realize that's what I was doing. I was so hungry to be in God's house, in His presence. I just wanted to be involved in the Kingdom in any way that I could, and my spirit was always crying out for whatever God had for me.

One of my favorite songs to sing as a young child was "Jesus, use me, and Oh, Lord, don't refuse me, for surely there's a work that I can do. And even though it's humble, Lord, help my will to crumble, and though the Cross be great, I'll work for you."

I remember being in missionary services, and feeling such an overwhelming heaviness, such a tugging in my spirit. I would weep and let God know that I was willing to go if that's what He desired me to do. And for a long time, I believed I had been feeling a missionary call.

However, around the age of nine or ten, the harder my shell became, the harder I found it to connect to God's presence.

Where I had once passionately sung my heart out, and praised and worshipped with all of my might, I began to stand rigidly in God's presence. It's not that I didn't want to be there, but as I began to give in to certain pressures from the world, I was ashamed and did not want to be hypocritical.

I lost that childlike wonder that I had always had of God, that feeling of adoration in His presence. His presence was there, but I was no longer being drawn in the same way.

I began losing the strong confidence in the natural giftings that God had blessed me with, and whenever I had the opportunity to sing (which was no longer as much), I could hardly sing without my voice shaking to death.

I had a few friends in junior high, and I started to feel the pull of peer pressure and the desire to fit in, although I had never before been ashamed of standing out. On the other hand, I knew I wasn't living for God wholeheartedly anyway, so I figured I might as well try to have some fun.

I began changing my appearance, and I started cursing, listening to secular music, etc. Ironically, though, if you had asked me about my future plans, I would have said that I would live for God and that I wouldn't be ashamed to dress holy, even though I didn't understand holiness at the time.

The summer before high school, at age 14, two incredibly significant events happened that would set the course for my adult life.

The first thing that happened was meeting a handsome and intriguing 21-year-old Bible college student. He was invited to become our church's music director, and he traveled to my hometown every weekend to lead the choir and help with other departments.

The second thing happened soon after, which was while attending youth camp. I went to the altar one night and knelt on the floor. My experience did not initially seem to be spiritually monumental. I even questioned my effort to go to the altar because I felt incapable of receiving what I needed from God.

During this time I had more of a casualness or coolness in my approach, but at the same time, I lived with a deep sense of fear because I saw God as someone quick to judge me for not living as I believed I should.

I wanted my relationship with God to be renewed, but on my own, I couldn't break the hardness that had developed nor find the victory to change my wrong desires or behaviors.

At the altar that night, which I hadn't regularly frequented for a long time, I desired to let God know that I still wanted Him. I was letting Him know that even though I was struggling to be free, that I still loved Him more than anything, and that I still desired to give my life to Him.

All of a sudden, I was given a vision. In this vision, God showed me two worlds, and I knew that He was showing me His Kingdom, and the kingdom of the world. Then, He spoke four words to me: "It's time to choose."

I fully perceived the message in the vision, and I immediately acknowledged that I would choose His Kingdom.

I did not have a good foundation of teaching, but I knew there was no option when given the choice so clearly. There was only one worthy choice.

I went home and got rid of all of the worldly apparel I had accumulated. I cleaned up my music, my language, etc. After moving into high school, I no longer had any friends for different reasons, and I felt more alone than ever.

The situation at home never improved. My dad viewed us from the lens of a depraved mind and assumed that we all had the same dark tendencies as he did.

For instance, he didn't like to allow my mom to see her family, and he accused her of seeking unnatural relationships with her brothers. He frequently accused her of desiring relationships with other men, even when she wasn't allowed freedom and had no opportunity.

When I was eight, my parents adopted a close family member. She was three. She couldn't comprehend where her mother had gone and why she couldn't see her anymore. She would cry uncontrollably every night for her mom.

My dad would go into a fit of rage and would beat and yell at her, telling her how ungrateful she was that we "took her in." He never comforted her in any way. I don't believe he was humanly capable of even attempting to understand the emotional pain she was suffering from no longer having her mom around.

He liked to claim that he had "rescued" her, but it seemed that he had an extra hatred for her. He was usually never fair or just in assessments of situations or us, but I noticed that he appeared to treat her more cruelly.

I will never forget the first few times I laid eyes on my ex-husband (again, he was 21, and I was 14). I remember well the attention he paid me, even in front of others at church. The looks. The stares.

The comments he made to let me know that he couldn't yet directly divulge how he felt because not everyone would "understand."

I believed that his attention was "special," but I didn't recognize that his looks were lewd, not typical, youthful admiration.

One day not long after I met him, he showed up at my house on my mother's birthday with flowers and a birthday cake, to wish her a "Happy Birthday." After he left, however, my dad said, "He didn't come to wish anyone a Happy Birthday; he came to see my daughter."

My mom and I tried to refute what my dad was saying, but I was secretly pleased because it meant that I hadn't imagined his attentions. Girls from the Bible college would come to see him at church youth functions, and I was so jealous because I thought they liked him, and that he might like one of them. This made me think that maybe I imagined his motives towards me, after all.

I found out later that he had a reputation for refusing to date anyone at Bible college, and his reasoning was because there wasn't anyone who met his "standards."

I usually didn't get to go out to eat with the youth on Sunday nights, but one evening I managed to get to go. He and another young man were the only two youth with vehicles, and there were just a few of us, so we would all ride together.

Incidentally, I was the only one that rode with "him," while everyone else rode in the other vehicle. They recognized his "focus" on me and wanted to allow us time to be alone.

This particular evening, while he was driving me home, it finally happened. I received the confirmation that I had been seeking. He told me directly that he liked me, but he admitted that there could be "issues," because not everyone would view it as an acceptable relationship. The reason for that eluded me at the time.

We began our limited dating experience shortly after I turned 15. My mom and dad allowed us to talk on the phone, and they let him come over and visit.

Not long before I turned 16, we were allowed to go to his company dinner without chaperone, and that began the next phase of our dating relationship.

Early on in our relationship, we began to encounter opposition, but not the kind we should have. The issues that my dad vocalized about him included his perceived lack of manliness due to his smaller size.

Of course, because I viewed my father as a real-life monster, and with my newfound boyfriend's ability to brim with love and charm, I considered my father's opinion to be shallow and lacking the perception to see "the real man.

The rest of the opposition we faced mostly dealt with my age, when we decided to get married. By that time, he was 23, and I was barely 16. The concern about my age that I received had nothing to do with my age versus his age.

Concerns were expressed that marriage could keep me from enjoying my youth and that my likes and dislikes would change as I got older. Of course, these were understandable considerations, but they did not bring attention to the true reason why I should not have married him.

I did not realize that I was the prey, marrying my predator. Because he married me, even many years later when beginning to comprehend his level of perversion, I still did not understand that I had been a victim of abuse.

I will not share stark details of my victimization. I will divulge, however, that he found ways to abuse me, against my wishes, right under my parent's noses.

I, unfortunately, did not realize that I was being abused. He was my boyfriend, after all. I knew that it was wrong behavior, but I didn't understand his violation or intrusion of me, even at a basic level.

I didn't realize that he could (and should) have gone to jail due to our ages. I couldn't comprehend the disrespect or violation of me that he was displaying by ignoring my wishes for him to stop. I was incapable of recognizing that his actions in no way expressed love, but dark lust. He was 22, and I was 15 when this began.

Suffice it to say that dreams of wedded bliss were not a reality for me. I quickly woke up to realize that my dream was a living nightmare, and I couldn't escape.

I was barely 17. I had only completed the first half of my junior year. I immediately became pregnant with my first child, and sickness began keeping me out of school. I tried homeschooling myself, but I wasn't disciplined enough. (I did end up finishing my schooling and getting my high school diploma three years later, through a self-paced preparatory school).

The first few years of our marriage, what most stands out in my mind was how he quickly became the opposite of what he had appeared to be. No longer the "happy-go-lucky," affectionate guy, he became sullen and angry, critical and derogatory, insulting and belittling me for any and everything.

He constantly made me feel like I was not good enough or intelligent enough for him. On one hand, he would be helpful by showing me how to do something I didn't know how to do, but he would severely criticize me for not doing it exactly like he thought it should be done. He treated me like a child, but in a way that even a child shouldn't be treated.

One instance that still stands out in my mind so dramatically involved me beating eggs for breakfast. Instead of simply telling me that I needed to beat them more, he spoke condescendingly to me like I was the most stupid person in the world. I remember thinking that no matter how knowledgeable he was, I would do my best to refrain from asking him for help in the future.

Even though this scenario played out in many different ways, it all had the same effect. I was at a place in life where I thought I could finally find peace and overcome my past, but my identity and sense of self-worth were only being further destroyed.

When he got home from work in the evenings, I would inevitably attempt to get a hug from him, and he would inevitably push me away. This pattern continued for many years.

He wanted us to go to bed together at night, but he would immediately turn over, refusing to express the most basic affections or love. I cried many nights over his rejection. I eventually began staying up far into the night to avoid facing his final rejection of the day.

I thought I had found love. I thought I would finally have a happy family. I thought I would have a secure home in which to raise my children. Sure, I had the basic provisions needed, but that does not make up for the lack of love or acceptance. That brings no comfort when your daily existence is riddled with torment.

I knew that I had no other place to turn than to God. I was so desperately empty, and beyond broken. My emotional condition made me question whether God's Spirit even still lived inside of me. It felt that no matter how much I cried out in God's presence, or sought to be changed, the vacuum inside only grew more and more profound.

I was oppressed. Depressed. Repressed. I had undiagnosed health issues, and in my early 20's, I lost weight that I couldn't afford to lose, and people told me I looked anorexic. I wasn't, but looking back at pictures I can see the stark gauntness in my face, and unwell appearance.

I did not feel well for most of my first pregnancy, and spent most of it sleeping. I thought this was normal, but after my daughter was born, I began to battle unimaginable fatigue.

Every morning was a fierce struggle to make myself get out of bed and take care of my daughter. I felt like a walking zombie, sludging through every day.

This was only the beginning of debilitating health issues that would eventually develop into Fibromyalgia in my 30's, and into my body beginning to shut down physically.

I knew that I could not give up. I knew that I could not turn to substances or the world. I believed in supernatural healing, and I knew that God could heal me emotionally as well as physically.

My kids were what kept me going. I had a strong desire to invest in their spiritual well-being, and I did not want them to have the same experience as me.

I wanted my children to have a balanced view of God's Word. I wanted them to love God and have a healthy reverence for Him. I did not want them running from Him and the church as soon as they had the opportunity.

I used every opportunity that I could as a teaching moment or lesson. I wanted to instill and invest wisdom of the principles behind the "why." I didn't want to teach my children to have the form, but not the substance.

A few years ago, after my second marriage, my health deteriorated to the point that my body was beginning to shut down. I was diagnosed with Fibromyalgia, anemia, and asthma. Through a process, I realized that I had been asthmatic and anemic all of my life, and going untreated for so many years created a multitude of issues.

My list of symptoms that I had dealt with for years was long, and the list was growing. In addition to the severe fatigue I mentioned, I also dealt with severe weakness, to the point that I felt like I would pass out most of the time. Many times this also caused feelings of light-headedness.

I dealt with severe heart palpitations, which added to the constant feeling that I would pass out. Then, in my early 30's, I began to ache and have pain all over my body. It felt like I had a steady case of the worst case of the flu.

Thankfully, by this time, my kids were older and becoming more self-reliant. They were accustomed to me cooking big meals every night, but it got to the point where I cooked less and less. I was involved in church, and I took care of my family as best as I could.

However, even that was a tremendous struggle, and I otherwise had to limit my effort towards other activities.

My body got into a routine. On the weekends, when I was a little busier, I would be out and about a little more, although I tried as much as possible to limit myself. On Sundays, I did not hold back in my singing and worship, no matter that every second to exert myself was a struggle.

Our church has an hour of Sunday school, followed by at least a two-hour service. I was already living in a physically depleted state, and by the time service was out, the thought of going home to cook was beyond overwhelming.

Sunday and Monday began a few days of extremely high pain levels, fatigue, and what I describe as my body shutting down. The achiness from Fibromyalgia grew to a level of severity, that it felt as if someone injected me with hard concrete from my neck all the way down.

Each day a considerable portion of my time was spent unable to get out of bed. Even sitting up and reading was out of the question. Later in the afternoon, I would finally be able to get up to try and tackle a few chores and possibly dinner. However, it constantly plagued me that my limitations were so significant. More and more, I had to choose which few areas to focus on, and I still struggled to accomplish even a few minor things.

Not long after I remarried, and began going to my new church, I focused heavily on praying for healing. Most people at my new church didn't know my struggles, but one Sunday, a sister who has now prophetically spoken into my life several times, told me that God was going to heal me.

However, she said that I needed more than physical healing and that I also needed emotional and spiritual healing. She also told me that it was my burden for my kids that would end up bringing it about, which I didn't understand at the time.

I now realize that in seeking a solid foundation and different futures for my children, the same was being created for myself. I definitely desired this for myself as well, but do not know if I would have had the strength to push as hard without being motivated by their lives.

As stated earlier, as a young married woman, I quickly realized that my dreams of happily ever after were not to be fulfilled. Naturally, I hoped that he would change, but of course, God does not force anyone to seek deliverance.

The first few years of our marriage were traumatizing, but I had no idea how genuinely horrific they would become. Initially, most of the abuse was mental, but there had also been some physical abuse, including when I was pregnant with my first child.

He never hit me, but he would push me around, and I was often scared that he would completely lose control. He loved to get right in my face while in a rage to try and control me. He did not like it when I did not cower to him.

For the first several years of our marriage, I was aware that he stared brashly at other girls, (even though he would vehemently deny it), but I still did not realize that I was married to a man with a perverse addiction.

We would get into terrible fights, because while he liked to look longingly at other girls, he no longer showed me any admiration. To the contrary, he rejected me outrightly every day.

My life up until this point had already overflowed with deep trauma and pain, but I was about to experience suffering that I never knew could exist.

Just six short years after saying "I do" to the man of my nightmares, with three small, innocent children, a close young relative came to live with us. For the purposes of this book, I will call her "Michelle." My ex was 30, and she was just shy of turning 18.

I want to state that I have never put the same level of blame on her for this situation that I did on him. I knew what he had done to me and how he had victimized me, (even though I still didn't fully grasp the depths of it), and I became convinced that he took advantage of her youth, vulnerability, and lack of a wholesome father figure.

During the time she lived with us, I dealt with feeling a lot of jealousy. He liked to spend time with her and sing with her, even though he wouldn't sing with me. He treated her kindly, while daily continuing to treat me with disdain. I thought his behavior stemmed from the facade he wore in front of others. I had no insight into his intentions.

She was great with the kids, and they had lots of fun with her, so I decided to take an out-of-state trip for a special occasion. My ex could not make the trip, and she offered to keep the kids, so I was free to go!

I was gone for an entire week. Around this time, I began working a few days a week at a local grocery store, and she babysat the kids.

I usually had to walk to work, but my ex would be home when I got off, so he would pick me up. One day, just a few weeks after I had gotten home from my trip, Michelle began to ask me questions about some physical issues she was having.

Her questions began to get more specific, and she would ask me if it was natural to skip your monthly cycle. At first, I thought she was becoming acclimated to female issues, and her questions didn't worry me.

As difficult as my marriage was, and as much as we fought, we prided ourselves on one thing. We refused to say the "D" word. DIVORCE. No, no, no, we did not believe in divorce. You wouldn't catch US threatening to get a divorce.

However, around the time that Michelle was having health issues, my ex and I got into a massive fight after church one Sunday because I dared to question him about the finances.

I knew better than to ask questions, but I always knew that something was wrong, and sometimes I just had to speak up. I now know that he was defensive because he was using our money in ways that betrayed our marriage.

This particular Sunday, while we were arguing about the finances and why they never made sense, he suddenly threatened to get a divorce. He told me in no uncertain terms that I would not be able to get custody of the kids because I could not afford to support them.

I was utterly shocked. I thought my ex had at least some integrity and that one day he would become a man who could treat his family with love and respect.

My ex had a very abusive father, and he had spoken many times of not wanting to become like him, and I sincerely thought that he cared about being a better man. So I could not believe that he was threatening to divorce me over an argument.

I went home extremely upset and called a friend from church. She knew of many of our problems, and she told me that day that if I ever needed a place to go, to not hesitate to call her. I had no idea of how soon I would have to accept that offer.

Just two weeks later, Michelle was complaining about not feeling good, and said that she needed to go to the doctor. I was on the phone with my ex, and he told me that he needed to talk to her.

Initially, I thought it was strange, but then I had a gut feeling that something was very wrong. I can still feel the sickening feeling in the pit of my stomach when I tell this story.

That evening I went to work, and my ex took Michelle to a clinic. All evening I could not get away from the feeling of knowing that she was most likely pregnant.

I was trying to think of who the father could be, and my mind did not want to venture into the possibility that it could be my husband.

When my ex picked me up, I asked how Michelle was doing. He said she was not doing good. I said, "She's pregnant, isn't she?" He answered affirmatively.

As my stomach churned, I asked who the father was, but I knew the answer before he gave it. He said, "It's me."

Before I could respond, he told me that he wanted us to talk. I told him that there was nothing to discuss and that I just wanted to go home, get my kids, and leave.

We lived close to a beach at that time, and he frantically drove to the park overlooking the beach. He quickly pulled up to the very edge of the concrete, and aggressively hit the brake just shy of the edge. I remember wondering if he had any thought of killing us both that night.

I cannot explain the rawness of the pain that I was feeling, nor the anxiety of what this meant. He kept begging to talk about it, and to know what I was thinking, but I kept reiterating that there was no point in me telling him what I thought of him. I just wanted out of the situation.

He said that he had already spoken to our pastor, and that we could "work this out." I knew, however, that any remorse came from getting caught and that word getting out would mar his image (and that was what he truly cared about).

I have since realized that "working things out" meant despite any actual change taking place, or no matter how damaging the behavior of the offending spouse.

My ex finally relented, and we went home. I called my friends and told them that we had to get out. I gathered clothing and necessities, and we left.

For the next couple of months, we lived with two different church families. I was staunchly against reconciliation, even though my ex was trying his best to get me to come back to him. I was being influenced by two different groups of people (each included friends and those in leadership) trying to persuade me in what they believed my course of action should be.

I truly wanted God's will, and what was best for my children. I did not want them to come from a broken home. I still did not understand the depth of my ex's sexual perversity, nor how it would eventually rear its ugly head yet again and cause even more significant damage.

I did not comprehend how broken my ex was, and still held out hope that things would improve. I knew that I had to forgive no matter what, but did that automatically mean that I had to reconcile? I understood that God always seeks reconciliation, and that he is against divorce, but I knew he also makes an exception for adultery.

I was so torn. On one hand, I was being advised that I had to forgive and reconcile. On the other, I was being told indirectly how stupid I would be, and to not be surprised when no one wanted to help me in the future if I reconciled.

The thought of reconciliation repulsed me because of his infidelity and continually severe treatment towards the kids and me.

My kids did not understand our separation. My daughter, who was the oldest at six, would question why we could not get back together. My ex told her that he wanted to reconcile but that I was the one who insisted on the separation. How do you explain such issues to such innocence?

I finally explained that her father had decided he loved another lady more than he loved her mom. I was at a loss on how to navigate such sensitive circumstances. It seemed that many wanted to judge me for how I did or didn't choose to handle the situation.

Some were kindly trying to support me, but I felt so much pressure from people's opinions. I also somehow felt that my situation was my fault. How could I be married to a man who would stoop to this kind of degradation? I now understand my naivety and realize that I was undoubtedly the object of hidden scorn in some instances.

It was at this time that I found out about his addiction to pornography. He fought to justify his actions by blaming this "weakness," but swore that he wanted to be a better man, husband, and father. He played on my sympathies, and stated that if anyone could forgive and overcome this betrayal, it was me.

I did believe that deep down there was a part of him that cared. The night I decided to reconcile, he broke down for several hours, shaking all over and sobbing. I have never seen the display of brokenness that I witnessed that night. He promised to change and to be the man that we needed him to be.

Unfortunately, in addition to his usage of pornography, and his highly selfish and cruel behavior towards myself and our kids, he also dealt with pride and arrogance that didn't typically allow him to address or admit any shortcomings. And if he did admit to anything, it was only to appease you temporarily.

He did try for a short while to be "on his best behavior." However, it didn't take long for his poor treatment of us to return, and six months after we reconciled, he lost a job due to pornography being found on his office computer.

Since I had discovered his propensity to look at porn ten years before, I blamed myself. I thought that if only I were prettier, more alluring, or had a fuller figure, he wouldn't desire to seek out women from a magazine.

I couldn't understand why he continuously rejected me. I did all I could to be a good wife. I expressed to him through the years that his viewing of pornography displayed unfaithfulness and was unacceptable. However, I sincerely desired his ultimate deliverance. I told him bluntly in an email after I left that I believed he only loved body parts, not an actual person.

As my kids grew, so did my despair. Our oppression was almost tangible. I recently saw a couple of videos of myself taken within just a year or two before leaving, and the suffering on my face was stark.

For the next 10 years, I held tenuously onto hope. Daily I trudged through life against all odds, attempting to take the best care I could of my family, in the constant face of fear, coldness, and rejection.

In the months leading up to my decision to leave once and for all, our "home" was in greater turmoil than we had ever experienced. The anger and rage was escalating. His behavior was at a new boiling point, with him coming threateningly close to hitting or pushing me.

We had a huge altercation a few months leading up to my leaving. Spring break was approaching, and comments were made about going on a camping trip with family. He began to make plans with his sister who lived several hours away, but instead of discussing the plans with me, he would discuss them with our young preteen daughter.

I would discover later that he had been treating my daughter as a "surrogate spouse," also known as "emotional incest." These terms describe when a parent seeks to meet his or her emotional needs through the child.

My ex-husband had never respected or validated me as his wife, so I viewed his attention towards our daughter as simply his attempt to be a better father.

I began to realize that he was not going to change and that my sons were most likely going to end up just like him if he was allowed to continue his harsh and unloving treatment towards them. I realized that even if he weren't abusing our daughter, that he could be on the brink of it.

My ex had gotten a job that doubled his pay, and although our financial situation did improve somewhat, we were still constantly behind on car payments and housing. Any time I tried to address the issue, he became irate. Then, a few months before I left, I found out about a secret bank account (that there was no explanation for) and began to suspect that he was doing things "on the side."

I began to pray and fast and confide in a few friends. Another close family member (unbeknownst to me) had previously asked my daughter about any potential abuse, and she denied it. Upon sharing my circumstances and fears with a few friends, they each encouraged me to talk to my daughter to see if she would open up once we left.

Open up she did, but only after knowing that her family breaking up wasn't her fault. She had been confiding in her best friend for several years, who had told her that sharing her secret would most likely result in her family being torn apart.

Unfortunately, she begged her young friend not to tell, and her friend didn't grasp the importance of going against her wishes.

As much as my heart had ever hurt, nothing hurt quite like my daughter detailing her abuse. At such a tender age, she had never been exposed to much in the ways of sexuality.

However, she would later be accused of lying by her father's family and by certain ones in spiritual authority. Many pieces of information from the past and present were consistently ignored. I was encouraged to reconcile and told that God could work out any situation.

Let me be clear that I believe that God CAN work out any situation, but God doesn't force change. Nor do I think he supports reconciliation in these situations, where this type of abuse is occurring.

The aftermath of our storm was horrific. Loss, harsh judgment, and rejection everywhere we turned. It was appalling that a child would be accused of lying in this manner. Who would desire to bear the stigmatization and ostracization of such events?

As a mother, I knew that my daughter had no desire to accuse anyone wrongfully. As past actions filtered through the knowledge of current situations, how could I ignore the glaring realization that my ex-husband didn't just have an unfaithful spirit? He was sexually deviant.

There are other issues I could share that caused me to realize that leaving was my only option. But, no matter the judgment or relationships lost that I experienced, I knew that I had to do what was right by my children before God.

I have never been the type to follow a particular direction because it is easy. Instead, I have always endeavored to do what is right, even if it costs me. Even if it's the road less traveled.

Being told that your husband must not be guilty or surely he would admit it is mind-blowing. Being told that your husband must not be guilty because the authorities couldn't convict him is laughable.

Criminals lie and get away with breaking the law all the time. The only reason he admitted what had happened ten years before was because the evidence couldn't be refuted.

The authorities did not question that the abuse had occurred, and if there were to be another formal complaint, he would be automatically arrested.

When confiding in certain spiritual elders about the porn issue, instead of addressing it truthfully as a genuine problem, in one instance I was told that whether or not it was an "addiction" couldn't be determined by someone who wasn't a psychologist or psychiatrist.

Another elder informed me, when I stated that I hadn't "signed up" to be married to someone who looks at pornography, said, "You didn't sign up to be married to a red-blooded male?"

It didn't seem to matter to many that our marriage shouldn't have occurred in the first place, and that there were signs from the beginning that my ex was sexually deviant.

It was simply my duty to pretend that these were normal issues that could be "worked out," no matter the boundaries that had been crossed, the damage that had been done, or even the proof that his behavior was deteriorating further.

How could I return my child to a situation that I now had a full understanding of?

Writing about these issues has been uncomprehendingly tough, but dealing with the past is crucial for healing to occur. In the world, and even in the church, many shameful circumstances are swept under the rug, without perpetrators having to face any accountability.

I realize that there are situations that are not beyond restoration, (such as infidelity), but God doesn't go against anyone's will. Because of the shame involved, it is easier to persuade the victims to hold their peace and stay in their situation. Pretend like horrific abuse doesn't take place within the confines of the church.

If a family appears "normal" from the outside, what does it matter the abuse that is perpetuated? That family will most likely pass some form of that abuse down to the next generation, despite the pleasant image they manage to maintain.

God revealed that there were generational curses (from both sides), and they had to be broken. So he took me through a process of awareness and then deliverance.

A part of that was removing my children from the destructive environment and allowing them time and space to heal.

Things were desperately rocky for a while, but we finally did get on our feet. My ex refused to allow me to access the bank account, nor would he voluntarily send any support for the kids, but God took care of us miraculously and blessed me with a good-paying job.

Looking back, I believe that all the signs pointed to my ex getting closer to furthering my daughter's abuse. God's hand had been leading me to escape, and once we left, the floodgates of Heaven opened.

God immediately began speaking to me through people who did not know our specific circumstances. I was told that my children would not be destroyed.

God spoke to me at the church that he directed me to one evening that I was beginning to act like a victim, even though I typically didn't have a victim's mentality.

The pastor said that as a sign to me that there was a light at the end of my tunnel, God would heal an infant that evening through my praying for her.

I prayed for the baby, not knowing what was wrong. I discovered later that the baby had "failure to thrive" syndrome, but that when the baby got home, it acted like a different child!

God knew that I desired to be more available for my kids, and my work schedule as a single mom was not the most convenient. I also longed for my children to witness a healthier marriage before they were fully grown, and so I prayed that God would bring the spouse He had for me. I did not trust myself to make that determination without His guidance.

Without a doubt, God brought another man into my life, preceded by specific prophecies, and followed by confirmations. He is a mighty man of God, loyal and faithful. Genuinely devoted to God, he is a man of prayer and a passionate worshiper. God told me that he would be faithful to me and that he would cherish me. And he has!

My kids and I finally had a peaceful home environment. Even though they have never called their stepdad "dad," his presence in their lives created an atmosphere of security.

Before leaving my ex, I had begun to have reason to believe that he had been doing other "things" outside of our marriage. About a year or so later a prophet of God confirmed that things took place all of those years that I never knew about.

The next several years were when my health began to decline drastically. My kids were graduating, getting jobs and vehicles, but it appeared that life had taken its toll upon me, and that there was no recovering.

Deep down, I did not believe that God was finished with me, but it seemed as if callings that I had had all my life would never come to pass due to health issues and emotional damage. I felt "ruined."

When I first began attending church with my new husband, I received two prophecies in the same service. Both prophecies were the same, and God told me that He would use my past circumstances as a "springboard" to use me in the way that He desired.

These messages were a reflourishing of hope, a rope to hold onto when these promises did not quickly come to pass.

In 2018, a friend (who I do not speak to regularly) heard about the LAMPS ministry. She was interested in seeing how it might help another friend of hers, but God spoke to her at the last minute and told her to invite me.

While there, I had a "feeling" that I would one day be involved in this ministry, but I was unsure if that was a word from God.

I had never heard of Sis. Kathy Corson or the LAMPS ministry. I was deeply ministered to at the service by several ladies. I only knew one of these ladies from my past. She was a radically different person from what I remembered, and I found out it was because of the LAMPS ministry. Her testimony is also in this book.

Sis. Corson told me that God was performing a deep-seated work and uprooting deeply ingrained hurt and pain from my past.

Sis. Karen Nichols told me that God was giving me a new heart and that he would restore my honor. She had no way of knowing the lies people believed about me and how that affected me.

Another sister shared that she could feel that God was about to use me in greater ways.

This was just the beginning of what God has spoken into my life the last few years. I can't begin to describe the impact that LAMPS has had on my healing journey.

I no longer feel that gaping emptiness. Strongholds are being broken. God has truly been making me whole and helping me to find my unique identity. He is preparing me to fulfill all of the lifelong callings I have had on my life. His favor rests upon me in a greater capacity than ever before.

Our visible and invisible wounds should deepen our focus, and create a more heartfelt compassion for others. It should also lessen our hastiness to judge others, or their circumstances. Situations are not always what they appear.

Releasing negative emotions and skewed perspectives releases us to be in a position to administer supernatural healing with God's help.

God has revealed that it is His will that I not only receive the healing that I need from LAMPS, but that He desires me to dedicate myself to its purpose.

He told me that my testimony will not go to waste and that LAMPS is the avenue by which I will seek to minister to others who are hurting.

He will use my talents, giftings, and unique experiences to minister specifically to those broken, seemingly beyond repair. My identity, confidence, worth, security, and sense of personality may have been destroyed before they even had a chance to develop, but these things can only truly be discovered in and through HIM. Who did He create us to be, and for what purpose?

As God has been performing a work of healing and wholeness in my life, I have begun to rediscover these vital aspects of myself in a whole new light.

I am discovering through experience, and not just through head knowledge, that what the enemy meant for evil, God really has meant for good. My identity is being recovered, and my purpose for God's Kingdom is being restored. I have found my confidence anew. It is not in me, but it is solely in the one who gave me anything I have in the first place.

My confidence is not dependent upon my ability, personality, or worth, but it is upon who I am in Jesus, and the anointing upon whatever I have consecrated to Him.

Recovering our identity in Jesus Christ means that our pasts do not identify us. Our mistakes nor our pain identify us. The process of healing enables us to walk the path that God has ordained for us. It releases us from being held back due to our past, or the opinions of others.

I am thankful to say that my children are all doing well. Each of them is now grown and on their own, working hard, and faithful to God's house. They are each growing spiritually, involved in ministries at church, and have a passion for souls.

I am not claiming responsibility. I know I sought to do my part to obey the admonishment of scripture, but I know that every person is ultimately accountable for their own decisions. Many have chosen not to follow God even when being raised in the best of homes. If you have a child that no longer lives for God, don't give up hope. All of the seeds you have planted are not in vain.

I have experienced deep healing in the last few years. My body no longer shuts down like it used to, and while I still limit myself physically, I am getting stronger every day. The physical issues that I have dealt with for years have gradually lessened.

I encourage you to attend a LAMPS service if at all possible, or to have your local church host one. It is a Spirit-led ministry. Sis. Corson is mightily used in the Gifts of the Spirit, and she is careful in ministering to others. She does not force anyone to respond, nor does she abuse the use of her gifts or callings. If you are ready to be deeply ministered to, the hand of God is ready to transform you wholly and powerfully.

I am eternally thankful to God for Sis. Corson and the ministry of LAMPS. It is truly an avenue by which one can receive miraculous emotional and spiritual healing. The Old Testament scripture found in Psalms 147:3 is still applicable today: "He healeth the broken in heart, and bindeth up their wounds."

Chapter 13 by D.S.

Scars

In Ecclesiastes 10:2, we read, "A wise man's heart is at his right hand; but a fool's heart at his left." Simply put, one cannot choose life's circumstances but can still determine one's perspective and reaction.

The acronym SCARS speaks to the lifelong journey of healing, restoration, and discovering who God created us to be. God forges his most prized jewels despite unplanned and unexpected life events.

The acronym SCARS represents: Secrets of the heart, Character of lives, Accepting promises, Realizing hope, and Seeking dreams and visions for lives. Scars develop in a lifelong process, and there is not an instant remedy.

Microwaves don't work on broken hearts and spirits. The children's song "He's Still Working on Me" illustrates the journey throughout life, becoming who God intended us to become.

Experienced artisans have restored valuable works of art, fine china, antique furniture, and historical documents. With great care and proficient skill, they labor for extended periods, meticulously restoring items to their intended priceless beauty. Only gifted, seasoned experts can see the remnants of any previous flaws or scars. The expert craftsman has skillfully covered any blemishes or discoloration from the artist's initially intended beauty.

Our Lord and Savior, Jesus Christ, is the Master Craftsman. He is keenly aware of the slightest hairline seams and fractures. He is attentive of every tiny ripple, scar or hidden flaw. He uses these very inconsistencies to kindle compassion never previously possessed.

Throughout life, traumatic events produce lifelong consequences, especially when experienced very young in life. The challenges faced by those who have endured such profound trauma are extensive.

People usually respond to traumatic events in one of two ways: through suppression and denial of events, and attempting to ignore the wounds and trauma suffered long ago in their lives, or by bravely facing it and acknowledging unjust and unfair treatment. These boldly bring their hurt and scars of the past and lay them down in submission to the Cross.

I cannot say that bringing painful memories of my past to the Lord has been a single, one-time event. Old memories creep in at strange times. When I thought I had conquered them, some simple reminder came along to dredge up the past.

Hearts, minds, and lives are like a living tape recorder. Our consciousness holds on to every sight, sound, feeling, smell, and taste. Sometimes when these senses are triggered, I find myself reliving an event, fully aware of the emotional scars created. Like grief, it comes in waves, usually around holidays or family events.

For myself, I find some alone time with the Lord and allow myself to grieve. Long after recovery of the physical scars, there needs to be time allowed for the heart, spirit, and mind to heal.

Trusting the Lord to guide me from mountaintop to mountaintop has been my lifelong source of strength, for I know that no matter how deep and long the valley is, God will eventually lead me back to the mountaintop again. I am never out of His sight. He has never once stopped loving me, guiding me, and sustaining me.

The verse in Ecclesiastes 10:2 defines which direction to choose in addressing the recovery process. In presenting the unwise heart, using the SCARS acronym, the correlation is clear. The Lord sees the secrets of the heart that remain broken, wounded, and crushed. But He is waiting for the marred to bring their wounds, pain, and scars to him. By holding onto the pain, the temptation is to withdraw from the only one who can heal the broken heart. Jesus is the healer of broken hearts.

Broken individuals live out their lives in a dysfunctional manner; while present in a crowd, they feel distant and alone. It is as if they are frozen in time, linked to brokenness, and not reaching out to the Lord to provide a more abundant life. The Lord is patient and kind but will not force the process of healing restoration. However, He will immediately respond to the faintest cry for His help and direction.

Accepting promises from the Lord is challenging after a lifetime of broken promises from people you once trusted. Broken promises contribute to a sense of skepticism in many, including in the Lord's devotedness and His abiding Word.

Take a step of faith, and courageously reach out to the only one who will never fail or give up on you. As guaranteed as the rising and setting of the sun, His Word is settled and sure. He doesn't change his mind based on what is popular in this ever-changing culture, nor does He forget His Word.

Realizing the gift of hope is a struggle to dare to believe and hope for positive changes and healing. But it is possible and achievable in the Lord. Invite the Lord to enlarge the boundaries in life, seeking new ways to find hope. Begin with small steps, such as hoping to wake up each morning. Life! It is the gift of God and a wonderful gift to anticipate!

Seeking dreams and visions is a final challenging hurdle to cross. After seeking the Lord, growing in restoration, gaining strength of character, knowing and accepting God's promises, and claiming the gift of hope, then pursue God's dreams, visions, and goals for life!

God knows who He created us to be, despite the enemy's attempt to distract and discourage us. Becoming God's chosen vessel of honor for His glory is the ultimate goal worthy of every challenge and effort made!

In presenting the wise man's heart, using the SCARS acronym, are the Secrets of the heart of those who seek out God's healing, restorative power. A broken heart knows healing is happening when the memories of the past do not hurt anymore. Turn to the only one who understands the wounded heart and can mend it by His divine power.

The Character of lives develops throughout the lifetime in the therapeutic process, growing more fully into the nature God envisioned when creating each one in the womb. Achieving God-given maturity of character is not a one-time remedy but is cultivated for a lifetime.

Accepting promises is claiming each assurance of the Lord as concrete evidence of His divine, unwavering love towards each one. It has confidence that whatever lies behind, and whatever lies ahead, God has already prepared the way. For every setback experienced, God has crafted a custom-made set-up for promotion and deliverance.

Realizing hope is never compromised or misleading when you secure your hope in the Lord. Life events experienced may have included major pitfalls of losing hope in others, but never in the Lord. As with the crashing waves of the ocean, God's tender mercies never fail. His love and faithfulness are absolute, giving us great confidence in putting our hope in Jesus.

Seeking dreams and visions come naturally as part of the restoration process and healing of past events. When the heart, spirit, and mind are free, the pursuit of dreams and visions for a bright future is a divine result. God's Word gives direction concerning seeking his visions and plans for the future.

In Jeremiah 29:11-14a, we read, "For I know the thoughts that I think toward you," saith the Lord, "thoughts of peace, and not of evil, to give you an expected end. Then shall ye call upon me, and ye shall go and pray unto me, and I will hearken unto you. And ye shall seek me, and find me, when ye shall search for me with all your heart. And I will be found of you, saith the Lord: and I will turn away your captivity, and I will gather you…"

As found in LAMPS meetings, restoration among sisters of like precious faith, hearts are invited, yes, encouraged to seek healing and Godly virtues of renewal and hope. Attendees represent different backgrounds and circumstances but jointly fit together by the unseen hand of God. In the depths of hearts that only God can see, participants experience an opportunity to release their hurts of yesterdays, to embrace God's goodness of each new day.

My testimony of attending LAMPS conferences was a moment in time of great enlightenment! I was not alone! I was in a safe, Godly, loving, and yes, hope-filled room with many others who had walked down that long, winding road to restoration. If you haven't visited a LAMPS service yet, please make arrangements to attend one soon. It is an encounter that could change your life forever!

Recovery from the scars of the past is often on the road less traveled. But the rewards awaiting those who bravely venture the risk of change are met with an overwhelming sense of peace, wholeness, and completeness found only in Jesus.

We could not find freedom of security in past chapters of our lives, but it now surrounds us in our daily walk. We have escaped the valley of death's shadow into the loving reverence, favor, and grace of God! May the Lord hold you, surround you, and lead every reader to the fullness of God's plan for your lives in Jesus' Name!

Rev. Kathy McManus Corson

Kathy McManus Corson is a U.P.C.I. licensed minister and resides in Summit, MS, with her husband, Rev. D. C. Corson.

She has devoted her life to full-time ministry, and she and her husband are both currently full-time evangelists. She was co-Pastor with her husband in Gibsland, LA, until the call of God to return to full-time evangelism.

She founded and directed specialized women's ministries such as God's Women and Weapons of War, a ministry to prepare and equip women to find their place in the Body of Christ for such a time as this.

She also established the LAMPS Ministry featured in this book, which focuses on becoming spiritually and emotionally whole to fulfill God's plan for your life

She has traveled extensively at the local, state, national, and international levels to proclaim the good news of Jesus Christ! She desires that the Kingdom of God come, and the will of God be done, on earth as it is in Heaven.

Her purpose is to fulfill Paul's goal of becoming all things to all men so that she might, by all means, win some!

Amber Nicole McKinzy

Amber "Nicole" McKinzy resides in Southeast Texas. She is happily married, and her three beautiful children are now grown and on their own. In the last couple of years, she has welcomed a most phenomenal daughter-in-law.

She is mainly called "Nicole," but is also called "Amber" by many, and she is "Nikki" to family and childhood friends. She eagerly awaits the day when she is called that most coveted name bestowed upon grandmothers.

Her lifelong desire has been to be a profound worshiper and fulfill God's plan for her life. Her passions include singing, writing/songwriting, reading, studying and expounding on God's Word, horseback riding, and nature. She loves to play various instruments and hopes to have more opportunity to practice now that her children are grown.

Nicole has always had a heart for ministry and is thankful for the opportunity to serve in whatever capacity God leads. She knows that her life and testimony will be used for the glory and kingdom of God.

Nicole is grateful for LAMPS and the impact it has had on her life, and she wholeheartedly believes that its legacy of changing lives is only just beginning.

Our Written Lives, LLC

Our Written Lives provides publishing services to authors in various educational, religious, and human service organizations.
For information, visit www.OurWrittenLives.com.

CPSIA information can be obtained
at www.ICGtesting.com
Printed in the USA
LVHW020025111121
702989LV00012B/486